MEET HENRI DE LUBAC

Rudolf Voderholzer

Meet Henri de Lubac

Translated by
Michael J. Miller, M.A.Theol.

IGNATIUS PRESS   SAN FRANCISCO

Original German edition
Henri de Lubac begegnen
Zeugen des Glaubens series
© 1999 by Sankt Ulrich Verlag, GmbH
Augsburg, Germany

Cover photograph of Henri de Lubac

Cover designer: Riz Boncan Marsella

ISBN 978-1-58617-128-5
Library of Congress Control Number 2006939359

Printed in the United States of America

CONTENTS

FOREWORD

"Never . . . have I found anyone with such a comprehensive theological and humanistic education as Balthasar and de Lubac, and I cannot even begin to say how much I owe to my encounter with them"—Cardinal Joseph Ratzinger, now Pope Benedict XVI.

Many have echoed then-Cardinal Ratzinger's judgment about the Swiss theologian Hans Urs von Balthasar and the French Jesuit theologian Henri de Lubac, S.J., whose life and work are described in the following pages.

It is perhaps not too soon to speak of the mid- and late-twentieth century as a modern "golden age" of Catholic theology. While Moehler, Newman and Scheeben are recognized as the most influential theologians of the nineteenth century, theologians of the late twentieth century built on and extended their achievements. To mention only the most obvious names: Louis Bouyer, Yves Congar, Karl Rahner, Hans Urs von Balthasar, Henri de Lubac and Joseph Ratzinger.

There were many others, of course, especially in more specialized disciplines such as liturgy, patristics, ecclesiastical history and exegesis. But I am referring here to what von Balthasar considered a theologian in the deepest sense: "one whose office and vocation it is to expound revelation in its fullness, and therefore whose work centers on dogmatic theology".

This description may not seem as applicable to Henri de Lubac as to the others I have named. But that is only because his ever-present interest in dogmatic theology was not expressed in treatises, much less manuals, but in more concrete forms such as historical studies.

De Lubac's contribution to theology and to the life of the Church was immense, as this biography will demonstrate. I count it as one of the great blessings of my life that as a young Jesuit I spent three years with him at the Jesuit theologate in Lyons, France, and acted as his assistant on the occasions when, because of illness, he needed help with his correspondence. I learned at first hand that he was not only a great scholar but an extraordinary person and priest, a man such as he himself describes in *The Splendor of the Church* as a *homo ecclesiasticus*, a man of the Church.

This was not just a blessing for me personally. It was because of my getting to know Father de Lubac, and through him Fathers von Balthasar, Bouyer and Ratzinger, that when I returned to the United States after my doctoral studies, I gathered together a group of collaborators to found Ignatius Press. The original vision was to make available to the English-speaking world the works of these great theologians.

Having translated and published many of the major works of Henri de Lubac, Ignatius Press is proud to publish now this biography, which will provide a wider context for the understanding and appreciation of those works.

The dedication I added to the Ignatius Press re-publication of Father de Lubac's classic, *The Splendor of the Church*, in the year of his ninetieth birthday, 1986, is even more appropriate now than it was twenty-two years ago:

> My personal debt of gratitude to this
> extraordinary scholar, loyal churchman,
> gracious and patient teacher, and fellow Jesuit
> is but a small part of what is owed him

by the countless numbers of men and women of every land
whose faith has been so profoundly enriched
by his life's work.

Cardinal de Lubac is above all else
a man of the Church, *homo ecclesiasticus*,
such as he himself portrays in these pages.
He has received all from the Church.
He has returned all to the Church.

This book, which, characteristically, he so humbly describes
in its introduction, is a testament that will endure
to his lifelong love of his Mother and ours,
the Immaculate Bride of the Lamb,
Holy Church.

—Joseph Fessio, S.J.
Editor, Ignatius Press

An Overview of the Life of Henri de Lubac

1896	February 20: Henri de Lubac was born in Cambrai, in northern France.
1913	October 9: entered the Society of Jesus. Made his novitiate at St Leonards-on-Sea, England.
1914	Drafted into military service.
1917	On All Saints' Day, November 1, he sustained a serious head injury.
1919–1920	Studied humanities in Canterbury.
1920–1923	Philosophical studies in Jersey, England.
1924–1926	Theological studies at Ore Place, Hastings, England.
1926–1928	Theological studies in Lyons-Fourvière, France.
1927	August 22: ordained a priest in Lyons.
1929	Instructor of fundamental theology at the Institut catholique (Catholic University) of Lyons.
1931	February 2: professed solemn vows as a Jesuit.
1934	Transferred to Lyons-Fourvière.
1938	Appointed professor of fundamental theology.
	Published *Catholicisme* (Eng. *Catholicism: Christ and the Common Destiny of Man*).
1939	Appointed professor of the history of religion.
1940–1944	Intellectual resistance against the National-Socialist regime.
1941	Founded the series *Sources chrétiennes*.
1944	Published *Corpus mysticum* (Eng. *The Mystical Body*) and *Le Drame de l'humanisme athée* (Eng. *The Drama of Atheist Humanism*).

1946	Published *Surnaturel*. De Lubac suspected of being an adherent of the *Nouvelle théologie* (New Theology).
1950	Published *L'intelligence de l'Écriture d'après Origène*.
	JUNE: Forbidden by his religious superiors to teach or publish. Transferred from Lyons to the Jesuit house in Paris on the Rue de Sèvres.
1950	AUGUST: Pope Pius XII published the encyclical *Humani generis*.
1951–1955	De Lubac's writings on Buddhism.
1953	Returned to Lyons (Rue Sala).
	Published *Méditation sur l'Église* (Eng. *Splendor of the Church*).
1956	Began working on the study *Exégèse médiévale*.
1958	Became a member of the Académie des sciences morales et politiques. Again permitted to teach and to publish theological works.
1960	Returned to Lyons-Fourvière.
	Invited to serve on the theological preparatory commission for the Second Vatican Council.
1962–1965	Named theological expert (*peritus*) at the Council.
	Defense of Teilhard de Chardin.
1963	Published commemorative three-volume collection of essays, *L'homme devant Dieu* (Man in the presence of God).
1969	Published *L'Église dans la crise actuelle* (The Church in the Current Crisis).
1969–1974	Member of the International Theological Commission.
1974	Published *Pic de la Mirandole*.
	After closing of Lyons-Fourvière, moved to Paris.

1976   Letter of thanks from Pope Paul VI on the occasion
            of de Lubac's eightieth birthday.

1979–1981   Published *La Postérité spirituelle de Joachim de Fiore*.

1983   FEBRUARY 2: created cardinal by Pope John Paul II.

1985   Published *Entretien autour de Vatican II* (Eng. *De
            Lubac: A Theologian Speaks*).

1988   Published *Résistance chrétienne à l'antisémitisme:
            Souvenirs 1940–1944* (Eng. *Theology in History: Part
            One: The Light of Christ; Part Two: Disputed Questions
            and Resistance to Nazism*).

1989   Published *Mémoire sur l'occasion de mes écrits* (Eng. *At
            the Service of the Church: Henri de Lubac Reflects on the
            Circumstances That Occasioned His Writings*).

1991   Henri de Lubac suffered a stroke that left him
            unable to speak. He died on September 4, after a
            difficult time of illness, in the care of the Little
            Sisters of the Poor in Paris.

ABBREVIATIONS

ASC   Henri de Lubac, *At the Service of the Church: Henri de Lubac Reflects on the Circumstances That Occasioned His Writings*, trans. Anne Elizabeth Englund (San Francisco: Ignatius Press, 1993).

AMT   Henri de Lubac, *Augustinianism and Modern Theology*, trans. Lancelot C. Sheppard (New York: Herder and Herder, 1969).

ATS   Henri de Lubac and Angelo Scola, *De Lubac: A Theologian Speaks* (Los Angeles: Twin Circle Pub. Co., 1985). (Abridged translation of *EVII*).

Cath   Henri de Lubac, *Catholicism: Christ and the Common Destiny of Man*, trans. Lancelot C. Sheppard and Elizabeth Englund (San Francisco: Ignatius Press, 1988).

CPM   Henri de Lubac, *The Church, Paradox and Mystery,* trans. James R. Dunne (Staten Island, N.Y.: Alba House, 1969).

CR   Henri de Lubac, *Christian Resistance to Anti-Semitism: Memories from 1940–1944*, trans. Elizabeth Englund (San Francisco: Ignatius Press, 1990).

DAH   Henri de Lubac, *The Drama of Atheist Humanism*, trans. Edith Riley, Anne Englund Nash, and Mark Sebanc (San Francisco: Ignatius Press, 1995).

DG   Henri de Lubac, *The Discovery of God*, trans. Alexander Dru (Grand Rapids, Mich.: Eerdmans, 1996).

DH   Denzinger/Hünermann, *Enchiridion symbolorum, definitionum et declarationum de rebus fidei et morum* [A compendium of creeds, doctrinal definitions and magisterial declarations on matters of faith and morals], Latin-German edition edited by Peter Hünermann (1991).

EVII   Henri de Lubac, *Entretien autour de Vatican II: Souvenirs et Réflexions* (Paris: France Catholique-Cerf, 1985).

HS   Henri de Lubac, *History and Spirit: The Understanding of Scripture according to Origen* (San Francisco: Ignatius Press, 2007).

MS   Henri de Lubac, *The Mystery of the Supernatural*, trans. Rosemary Sheed (New York: Herder and Herder, 1967).

Mystik   Henri de Lubac, "Christliche Mystik in Begegnung mit den Weltreligionen" [Christian mysticism in its encounter with world religions], in J. Sudbrack, ed., *Das Mysterium und die Mystik: Beiträge zu einer Theologie der christlichen Gotteserfahrung* (1974), pp. 77–110.

Lenk   Martin Lenk, *Von der Gotteserkenntnis: Natürliche Theologie im Werk Henri de Lubacs* (1993).

PF   Henri de Lubac, *Paradoxes of Faith* (San Francisco: Ignatius Press, 1987).

SpCh   Henri de Lubac, *The Splendor of the Church*, trans. Michael Mason (San Francisco: Ignatius Press, 1999).

PART ONE

STORY OF A THEOLOGIAN

The Cardinal

On September 16, 1991, the international weekly news-magazine *Time* reported:

> Cardinal Henri de Lubac, one of the top theologians among the French Jesuits, died at the age of 95 in Paris. De Lubac was prohibited from teaching from 1946 to 1954 after the publication of his book *Surnaturel*.[1] Rehabilitated in 1958, he took part in the [Second Vatican] Council at the request of John XXIII. His relations with Rome then became even more intensive during the reign of John Paul II, who, during a visit to Paris in 1980, interrupted a speech that he was giving when he saw the priest and said, "I bow my head to Father de Lubac."

In 1983, the Pope appointed the then eighty-seven-year-old theologian a cardinal in recognition of his services in the field of theology. This honor, which Henri de Lubac dedicated to the Jesuit Order as a whole, was the last step in the rehabilitation of a man who for a time was suspected, even within the Church, of watering down the true faith with all sorts of "innovations" and who from 1950 to 1958—here the *Time* report is inaccurate—was dismissed from his teaching

---

[1] De Lubac's controversial book *Surnaturel: Études historiques* (1946) unmasked the theory of *natura pura* as a theological construct from the modern period and thus presented a challenge to the foundations of the Neo-Scholastic theology taught in the schools. On this subject, see the detailed discussion, below, on pp. 63–64, 92, and 122–38.

position on the basis of such suspicions and was forbidden to publish scholarly books on theology.

Henri de Lubac and Karol Wojtyla, who later became Pope, were already acquainted from the days of the Second Vatican Council and held one another in high esteem. They had worked together on that "Schema 13" which eventually became known as the Pastoral Constitution on the Church in the Modern World, *Gaudium et spes*[2] (Joy and Hope). Even more than by his direct collaboration on the conciliar texts, de Lubac influenced the Council through the voluminous theological studies that he published in the years leading up to the Council, through which he had contributed to a renewal of theology based on the sources, that is, Sacred Scripture and the writings of the Church Fathers. Essential preliminary work for both the Dogmatic Constitution on the Church, *Lumen gentium*, and the Dogmatic Constitution on Divine Revelation, *Dei Verbum*, which are the most important theological documents of the Council, was done in the writings of Henri de Lubac.

For his part, Henri de Lubac recognized, in his encounters with the learned Archbishop of Krakow, that he was dealing with an extraordinary individual. The two became friends and corresponded. De Lubac wrote a foreword to the French translation of Wojtyla's book *Love and Responsibility*, while Wojtyla commissioned a Polish translation of de Lubac's essay *Églises particulières et Église universelle* [Motherhood of the Churches]. In 1970 and 1971, Wojtyla invited de Lubac to

[2] Conciliar texts, as well as other magisterial documents, are cited according to the words with which they begin in Latin: *Lumen gentium, Dei Verbum, Gaudium et spes*, etc. They can be found in *Documents of Vatican II*, ed. Austin P. Flannery (Grand Rapids, Mich.: Eerdmans, 1975); or in the more recent edition, *Vatican Council II: The Basic Sixteen Documents: Constitutions, Decrees, Declarations*, ed. Austin P. Flannery (Northport, N.Y.: Costello; and Dublin: Dominican Publications, 1996).

Poland. Only de Lubac's illness kept him from carrying out his travel plans. De Lubac recalled that in familiar conversations he had repeatedly made the assertion: "After Paul VI, Wojtyla is my candidate."

"A Genius for Friendship"

Anyone who undertakes to make a biographical sketch of Henri de Lubac is obliged in the first place to refer to the *Mémoire sur l'occasion de mes écrits*,[3] which he finally published in 1989 in the twilight years of his life; this "memorandum" is actually a report that he himself composed in several stages concerning the circumstances in which his writings originated. This book will always be an authoritative source for any in-depth study of the person and work of Henri de Lubac. During the years 1956 to 1957, de Lubac made notes about the first twenty years of his life, but he did not publish them.[4] An initial series of these memoirs has meanwhile been compiled from his literary remains, extensively annotated, and published by Georges Chantraine. De Lubac also recorded extensive memoirs of the years of World War II and the German occupation of France and published them in French in 1988.[5]

De Lubac always tried to keep his personal life in the background. This is true both of his writings and also of his

[3] Henri de Lubac, *Mémoire sur l'occasion de mes écrits* (1989); English edition, *At the Service of the Church: Henri de Lubac Reflects on the Circumstances That Occasioned His Writings*, trans. Anne Elizabeth Englund, Communio Books (San Francisco: Ignatius Press, 1993), here cited as *ASC*. This work contains autobiographical notes, along with a wealth of such material as book reviews, letters and diary entries.

[4] Henri de Lubac, "Mémoire sur mes vingt premières années" I, *Bulletin de l'Association Internationale Cardinal Henri de Lubac* 1 (1998): 7–31.

[5] Henri de Lubac, *Christian Resistance to Anti-Semitism: Memories from 1940–1944*, trans. Elizabeth Englund (San Francisco: Ignatius Press, 1990).

autobiographical memoirs. He never thought of his theology as being original. It is one of the ironies in the history of theology that he, of all people, should be described by his opponents as the spokesman of a supposedly "new theology", the *Nouvelle théologie*. "In his writings he carried this attitude [of objectivity] to the point of self-effacement; many pages penned by him are nothing but a tissue of quotations, interwoven with comments. He renounced a speculative theological *oeuvre* so as to be like that 'scribe who has been trained for the kingdom of heaven' who 'brings out of his treasure what is new and what is old' in extravagant abundance"—thus Xavier Tilliette described de Lubac's approach in an appreciation written on the occasion of the latter's eightieth birthday.[6] The principal motive of his academic work was to put in the proper light the truth of the faith and the beauty and splendor of Tradition, along with the life's work of his friends. Father Gerd Haeffner said that he had "a genius for friendship".[7] Many pages of his retrospective are devoted to the memory of confreres and friends. Besides his own nearly forty volumes, de Lubac published almost as many books by friends posthumously, besides writing forewords and introductions and editing and annotating correspondence. Henri de Lubac published seven voluminous manuscripts by Father Yves de Montcheuil, S.J. (b. 1899), who was murdered by the Nazis in Grenoble in August 1944 shortly before the liberation of France. It is true that the manuscripts were almost ready to go to press, yet de Lubac singlehandedly saved them from oblivion. He devoted three books on a grand scale to the defense of his confrere and friend Teilhard de Chardin (1881–

[6] Xavier Tilliette, "Henri de Lubac achtzigjährig", *Internationale Katholische Zeitschrift Communion* 5 (1976): 187f.

[7] Gerd Haeffner, "Henri de Lubac", in Stephan Pauly, ed., *Theologen unserer Zeit* (1997), pp. 47–57.

1955). It pained him that his plans to publish important works of Father Pierre Rousselot, S.J.,[8] who died in World War I at the age of thirty-seven, repeatedly came to naught!

Whereas he published and publicized the works of others, this same service was done for him by Hans Urs von Balthasar (1905–1988), one of his close friends from their days together in Lyons-Fourvière. As early as 1947, von Balthasar translated de Lubac's first book, *Catholicisme*.[9] Then, in 1967, he began to publish the collected works of de Lubac in German. These were published by Johannes Verlag, the publishing house he himself had founded and directed. Thus almost all of the principal works are available in German, in a suitable translation, thanks to the stylistic brilliance of Hans Urs von Balthasar. An abridged version of the four-volume *Exégèse médiévale*, which Henri de Lubac himself prepared under the title *L'Écriture dans la Tradition* (1966), has recently appeared in English as *Scripture in the Tradition*.[10]

Although the most important writings of Henri de Lubac are thus accessible to the German-speaking reader, they are actually known in Germany [and in the English-speaking

---

[8] Pierre Rousselot, S.J. (1878–1915), professor for dogmatic theology in Paris. His doctoral thesis, *L'Intellectualisme de saint Thomas*, a milestone in the recovery of Thomas' original views, had a decisive influence on de Lubac's approach to theology. On Rousselot, see E. Kunz, *Glaube, Gnade, Geschichte* [Faith, grace, history] (1969).

[9] Henri de Lubac, *Catholicisme: Les Aspects sociaux du dogme* (1938). Translated into German by Hans Urs von Balthasar as *Katholizismus als Gemeinschaft* [Catholicism as community] (1943); a second edition of this translation appeared in 1970 with the modified title *Glauben aus der Liebe* [Faith out of love]. English edition: *Catholicism: Christ and the Common Destiny of Man*, trans. Lancelot C. Sheppard and Elizabeth Englund (San Francisco: Ignatius Press, 1988), here cited as *Cath*.

[10] Henri de Lubac, *L'Écriture dans la Tradition* (1966); English edition, *Scripture in the Tradition*, trans. Luke O'Neill (New York: Crossroad Publishing, 2000); German edition, *Typologie, Allegorie, Geistiger Sinn*, trans. Rudolf Voderholzer (Einsiedeln: Johannes Verlag, 1999).

world] only by a limited circle of specialists—limited, when compared with the scope and significance of his work. Who, then, was Henri de Lubac? What are his most important works? When and in what connections were they produced? In what manner and through what insights did he prepare the way for the Second Vatican Council? What was his opinion of the postconciliar developments? On what theological topics does he have something of lasting value to say?

Formation

Henri de Lubac was born on February 20, 1896, in Cambrai, in northern France, the third of the six children of Maurice Sonier de Lubac (1860–1936) and Gabrielle de Beaurepaire (1867–1963). Although de Lubac's father was originally from the region south of Lyons, he worked for the Banque de France, which transferred him to positions in the east and north of France, in particular, to Cambrai during the years 1895–1898. According to Georges Chantraine,[1] there were other reasons behind this move. Pursuant to the law of March 29, 1880, members of religious communities were expelled from their houses and institutions. In Lyons the expulsion of the Capuchin Franciscans led to demonstrations on November 3, 1880, during which one protester was killed. De Lubac's father, together with some friends, was escorting the expelled friars and became involved in a brawl, during which he injured one of the counter-demonstrators slightly in the face with the pommel of a sword. For this he was sentenced to a jail term and fined sixteen francs. The court of appeals in Lyons recognized that he had acted in self-defense, but punished him for carrying an unauthorized weapon and upheld the fine. In the Sonier household, this judgment was regarded as an honor. Nevertheless, Maurice de Lubac thought it best to leave Lyons behind for the

---

[1] Georges Chantraine et al., eds., *Henri de Lubac: Mémoire sur mes vingt premières années*, p. 15, n. 16. This work was published posthumously with *Mémoire sur l'occasion des mes écrits* (Paris: Éditions du Cerf, 2006).

time being; eventually, in 1898 the entire family moved to Bourg-en-Bresse, and finally, in 1902, they returned to Lyons.

De Lubac writes about his parents and family in his memoirs, *At the Service of the Church.*

> My parents were hardly well-to-do. . . . They raised us according to the principles of a strict economy, but we were bathed in their tenderness. My mother was a simple woman. Her entire education was received in the country and in the cloister of a Visitation monastery, according to the custom of the times. Her entire upbringing rested on the foundation of Christian tradition and piety. I never saw anything in her but self-forgetfulness and goodness. After the death of my father, who had worn himself out in daily labor, she said to me one day, "We never had the least disagreement" (*ASC*, p. 152).

Childhood and School Days

Henri de Lubac spent his childhood in Bourg-en-Bresse and Lyons and received his primary education in various institutions run by religious orders: at first at the Christian Brothers' school in Bourg-en-Bresse in 1901–1902, and then at another in Lyons under the same auspices until 1904. In 1905 he transferred to the Jesuit-run Saint Joseph's Preparatory School in Lyons. From 1909 to 1911 he continued his studies at the Jesuit College of Notre Dame de Mongré in Villefranche-sur-Saône, some twenty-five kilometers north of Lyons, which was regarded as an elite institution. (A few years previously, in 1897, the young Teilhard de Chardin had graduated from Mongré with a stellar academic record.) Among de Lubac's favorite books while he was at school were works by the contemporary Catholic authors Charles

Péguy and Paul Claudel,[2] the Latin poet Virgil and also the Russian novelist Dostoyevsky. The time that he spent in Villefranche was very important for Henri de Lubac's subsequent career. Under the spiritual direction of Father Eugène Hains, S.J., whom he held in great esteem for the rest of his life, he discerned a vocation to a life of imitating Christ in a special way (*ASC*, p. 402). But the first item of business was to complete his schooling. Beginning in 1911, de Lubac studied at the College of Moulins Bellevue, earning the baccalaureate and thus a secondary school diploma in 1912. He enrolled for two semesters of law courses at the *Institut Catholique* of Lyons and then applied in the autumn of 1913 for admission to the Society of Jesus. He entered the novitiate[3] on October 9, 1913; at that time, however, the novitiate was not conducted in France, but rather in St Leonards-on-Sea, a suburb of Hastings, on the coast of the English Channel. During those years anyone who entered the Jesuit Province of Lyons, or one of the Order's three other French provinces, had to make his novitiate and pursue his studies in England; this was not for the purpose of gaining experience abroad, but rather for political reasons. This is typical of the situation of the Church in France during those years. It should always be kept in mind also as part of the background for understanding de Lubac's work. This factor has been labeled *la séparation*.

The Intellectual Climate

Séparation characterizes not only the relation between Church and State, from a political perspective, but also, intellectually,

---

[2] See Henri de Lubac and Jean Bastaire, *Claudel et Péguy* (1974).

[3] A novitiate serves as an introduction to the spirituality of a religious order and a time in which to discern one's own vocation in life.

the relation between philosophy and theology, and between the natural order and the supernatural order of grace.

Although France was once hailed as "the eldest daughter of the Church" because of her loyalty and close ties to Rome, developments during the eighteenth century, culminating in the French Revolution, left the relationship between Church and State in complete disarray. Catholics, and of course the nobility in particular, viewed all republican trends with profound suspicion, while conversely supporters of the French Republic were filled with a deep disdain, indeed, often an outright and passionate hatred for the Church and her institutions, especially for the Jesuit Order. Granted, Church-State relations had improved thanks to the Concordat of 1801–1802 and then again over the course of the nineteenth century after the Restoration of 1814–1815. The Society of Jesus[4] had been suppressed by Pope Clement XIV in 1773 and was not reestablished as an order until 1814; as of 1832 the Jesuits were able to gain a firmer footing again in France. The year 1850 brought the law granting full educational freedom and inaugurated a period of consolidation. Toward the end of the nineteenth century, however, tensions worsened again in every respect. As early as 1880, the Jesuits, too, not being a government-approved association, were once more deprived by law of the right to give instruction. Thirty-seven colleges were dissolved. Those who were expelled, some of them forcibly, traveled to England, Belgium or Spain, or else went to the missions. A remnant of the priests was able to stay in France. The general population in the staunchly traditional

---

[4] The Jesuit Order is actually named the Society of Jesus (*Societas Jesu*), abbreviated S.J. It was founded by Ignatius of Loyola (1491–1556) and received papal approval in 1540. Besides the three vows of poverty, chastity and obedience, members take a fourth vow: to go wherever the pope might send them for the salvation of souls.

regions in France, to be sure, was much better disposed toward the Jesuits than the legislature and regarded the law as invalid. Thus, shielded by public opinion, the work of teaching in the colleges could be continued to a limited extent.

The 1890s were characterized by efforts of Catholics with republican views to bring about a *rapprochement* with the State. Their policy of *ralliement* [reconciliation] was expressly promoted by Pope Leo XIII. Ultimately, though, it failed in 1898, and French society became increasingly polarized.

The Christian Democrats, who were not united among themselves, managed to win only a negligible number of seats in the elections of 1893 and 1898. In June of 1898, they were excluded from participating in the French government. On June 26, 1899, as Pierre Waldeck-Rousseau and his coalition of *la Concentration Républicaine* took charge of the government, a decidedly anticlerical program was set in motion.

The affair involving the French-Jewish artillery officer Alfred Dreyfus was a serious setback for the politics of reconciliation. He had been sentenced to lifelong deportation in 1894 on account of his alleged betrayal of military secrets to Germany. Waldeck-Rousseau allowed the case to be reopened. In 1899 that resulted, however, only in a reduction of the sentence and a pardon, not in an acquittal and rehabilitation (which came about only in 1906), and the Republicans tried to blame the unsatisfactory outcome on the influence of right-wing Catholics and their anti-Semitic tendencies. The politics of reconciliation failed, and the opposition between the anticlerical Republicans on the one side and the Catholic Church on the other became hardened, whereby the Catholic partisans themselves split into a national movement (*Action française*) and a smaller group that was open to democracy.

Émile Combes succeeded Waldeck-Rousseau in 1902 and continued his policies. During the years 1903–1904, twenty thousand religious were expelled from France, expulsions that occasioned popular protest demonstrations, for instance, in Lyons and Nantes, in the course of which there were fatalities. During the reign of Pope Pius X (1903–1914), diplomatic relations between the Holy See and the French government were broken off (1904), and in 1905 the Concordat that had regulated Church-State relations since 1801–1802 was abrogated. Even though it had given the government some say in ecclesiastical matters, the Concordat until then had granted the Church in France a certain scope of action and had guaranteed its financial support. By legislation passed on December 11, 1905, the complete separation of Church and State was sealed.

Thus separation at the intellectual level was accompanied by separation at the societal level. The separation on the intellectual level is the more fundamental of the two. It brought forth modern secularization, in the sense of a self-imposed restriction of the political and societal realm, which is walled off from any and all religious influence. De Lubac formulated the provocative thesis that modern philosophy is not exclusively to blame for this, but also theology itself through its sharp demarcation between the natural and the supernatural.[5] This insight emerging from the analyses of the book *Surnaturel* contained an enormous amount of explosive material and accordingly caused repercussions that burst upon the scene in the form of large-scale suspicions and accusations against de Lubac.

[5] See Henri de Lubac, *The Mystery of the Supernatural* [*Le Mystère du surnaturel* [1965]), trans. Rosemary Sheed (New York: Herder and Herder, 1967), pp. 239–40. Grace is a fundamental concept in theology. Grace is first of all God himself, who freely and undeservedly gives himself to his creatures in love (*uncreated grace*). We speak of *created grace* insofar as God establishes within a creature the conditions for accepting the divine gift. Concerning the book *The Mystery of the Supernatural*, see also p. 93, n. 16, below.

"Two-Story Thinking"

So there is *séparation* on the intellectual level as well. De Lubac speaks again and again about a *philosophie séparée* or a *théologie séparée*, expressions that are difficult to translate (literally: separated philosophy and separated theology). In the German language, it has become customary to use the metaphor "two-story thinking" to refer to what he means. This implies that the supernatural order of grace is abruptly added on to the natural order, without the possibility of demonstrating any intrinsic coordination of the two levels ("stories"). God's grace impels man, who has to accept this grace on the basis of divine authority. In order to preserve the gratuitous character of grace as a gift, the theology of *natura pura* [pure nature], which became generally accepted from the seventeenth century on, supposed that man is, in principle, perfectible even without grace in a state of natural happiness, which does not consist of the vision of God. Although theologians were still aware at first that this marked a departure from the tradition of Saint Thomas Aquinas[6] and of all Catholic theology before him, this notion was increasingly taken for granted from then on, and since the seventeenth century it has been thought to be the theology of Saint Thomas himself. This distinction between the natural and the supernatural, considered as two unassociated orders [of reality], was one of the pillars of the so-called Neo-Scholastic theology, which served as the textbook theology in Catholic seminaries and universities from the late nineteenth century on and also had Jesuit

---

[6] St. Thomas Aquinas (1225–1274), the most important theologian of the Scholastic period, was a Dominican friar and has been declared a Doctor of the Church. His philosophical and theological writings are very highly esteemed and have been recommended above all others for those who are studying Catholic theology.

and Dominican scholars among its leading proponents. Ever since Maurice Blondel expressly introduced the concept as a neologism in his book *History and Dogma* (1904), theologians have spoken in this connection about extrinsicism. This concept became widely accepted with astonishing rapidity. Overcoming extrinsicism is the basic concern about which Henri de Lubac, Karl Rahner[7] and many other twentieth-century theologians are in agreement. They characterized as extrinsicistic that understanding of revelation which maintains that God's self-communication encounters man completely "from outside" (*extrinsece*), without any possibility of clarifying, from the perspective of the one receiving revelation, to what extent he is disposed to receive it, that is, to what extent he is in principle a "hearer of the Word", as Karl Rahner would later put it.

Besides this separation between philosophy and theology, which was accompanied especially in the late nineteenth century by the tension between the natural sciences and theology, a second separation arose within theology itself on the basis of an even earlier parting of the ways: the separation between theology and spirituality.[8] De Lubac and many of his contemporaries were painfully aware of all these separations.

As for the separation between philosophy and theology, or between nature and grace, the true meaning of "catholic" begins to shine forth only against this background. Catholic, in the sense of "all-inclusive" or universal, essentially implies the removal of this separation, not in the sense of a cheap

---

[7] Karl Rahner, S.J. (1904–1984), was a professor of theology. On his life and work, see Michael Schulz, *Karl Rahner begegnen* (Sankt Ulrich Verlag, 1999). His book *Hörer des Wortes* [Hearers of the Word] has been published as volume 4 of the *Sämtliche Werke* [Complete works] of Karl Rahner.

[8] See Henri de Lubac, *AMT*, pp. 293–96. Originally published as *Augustinisme et Théologie moderne* (1965).

accommodation of the world, but rather in the sense of a view of man and society in the light of revelation, which responds to man's ultimate questions and the most profound "demands" of his spirit. True catholicity (as distinguished from Catholicism) leads to an image of man that elevates and perfects both the individual and society. To be Catholic means, not to deny reason, but rather to understand it as the antenna by means of which God's revelation can be received.[9]

All of the above-mentioned separations inevitably have very detrimental consequences on either side.

Modernism

In the years around the turn of the twentieth century, it was the concern of many Catholic intellectuals to meet the challenges of modern historical research (which meanwhile was playing a predominant role in so-called liberal Protestant theology), along with secularized philosophy and comparative religious studies, as well as the findings of the natural sciences, and not just to retreat to the safety of defined doctrinal statements of the faith. Not all of them succeeded in preserving intact the deposit of the faith and the principles of Catholic teaching. This brings up another keyword that requires explanation: *Modernism*. The term is a slogan that was used to characterize certain theological views, but it was often adopted by those in question to describe their own position. In the decree *Lamentabili*, dated July 6, 1907, and then especially in the encyclical by Pope Pius X, *Pascendi dominici gregis*, dated September 8, 1907, Modernism was systematically set

[9] Cf. Eugen Maier, *Einigung der Welt in Gott: Das Katholische bei Henri de Lubac* [The unification of the world in God: the concept of Catholicism in Henri de Lubac] (1983).

forth and condemned. The encyclical classifies as Modernist the stances of agnosticism[10] and immanentism,[11] the claim that Sacred Scripture contains errors as well as truth and, finally, the claim that the teaching of the faith has distanced itself from its biblical foundations over the course of time (discontinuity in doctrinal development). The main problem seems to have been an all-too-uncritical acceptance of historical-critical exegesis[12] and the attempt to play off its findings at that time against traditional Church teaching. It is generally agreed that the most important proponent of Modernism was the French exegete Alfred Loisy (1857–1940), who, in his book *L'Évangile et l'Église* (*The Gospel and the Church*), published in 1902, had attempted to defend the Catholic Church and her opinions concerning the origin of the Church in the public ministry of Jesus against Adolf von Harnack's critique in *Das Wesen des Christentums* (*What Is Christianity?*). "Jesus proclaimed the Good News about the Kingdom of God. But the Church came instead." This famous formula, which Loisy had not meant disparagingly, nevertheless failed to preserve the continuity between the Church and Jesus' public ministry, and thereby it had made too great a concession to Protestant exegesis. The introduction of the Oath against Modernism in 1910, which all clerics were obliged to take (until 1967), shows how dangerous a

[10] Agnosticism holds that human reason is incapable of lifting itself up to God and recognizing his existence from created things.

[11] Immanentism holds that religion springs from an "interior" (immanent) sense. According to this view, neither does revelation come to man "from outside" (from God).

[12] Historical-critical exegesis is the investigation of Sacred Scripture using the methods of historical and literary scholarship. Its origins in the seventeenth century were encumbered by the *deistic* denial of revelation. This objection concerns the philosophical foundations and the unwarranted conclusions of the approach, but not the method itself. See below, p. 197. On deism, see below, p. 161, n. 1.

threat Modernism was considered to be by the Church's Magisterium.

History and Dogma

The epoch-making work that finally broke the ground for a genuinely new encounter between the Church and the world was *L'Action*, by Maurice Blondel.[13] He submitted this study, which is somewhat comparable to an inaugural dissertation, to the faculty of philosophy at the Sorbonne in Paris in 1893. It demonstrated how the dynamic of human fulfillment in life through acts of reason and will aims beyond itself in such a way that it finally and necessarily inquires about the possibility of a revelation of God taking place in history.

Blondel, too, was suspected of Modernism, and his often sorrowful career was similar in many respects to de Lubac's. In fact, Blondel's *Histoire et Dogme* is probably the most solid and thorough treatment of one of the major problems of Modernism. In his debate with Harnack and Loisy, Blondel points out the philosophical presuppositions and the resultant "shortcomings" of a self-sufficient historical-critical exegesis.

Maurice Blondel was the standard-bearer and sign of hope for several generations of young Catholic intellectuals. *L'Action* was copied out by hand and circulated. Henri de Lubac, too, would find crucial inspiration in the writings of Maurice Blondel and would go on to lend theological support to the philosopher's fundamental thesis.[14] He transmitted to the field of theology the impulse that started with Blondel.

[13] Maurice Blondel (1861–1949) was a Catholic philosopher who taught in Aix-en-Provence. His doctoral dissertation was entitled *L'Action* (1893). In 1904, he published the book *Histoire et Dogme*.

[14] On Blondel and his relationship to Henri de Lubac, see Antonio Russo, *Teologia e dogma nella storia* (1990).

Through de Lubac, along with Pierre Rousselot (1878–1915) and Joseph Maréchal (1878–1944), German theology, too, was influenced—first and foremost Karl Rahner (1904-1984), whose accomplishment would be inconceivable without this preparatory work in France.

Thus we have sketched, in broad strokes, the backdrop against which the life and work of de Lubac was to be played out. His academic career was interrupted in 1914 by the war.

Wounded in War

Like most French clerics, de Lubac was drafted into the military service in 1914. From 1915 to 1918 he was stationed with the Third Infantry Regiment in Antibes, Cagnes-sur-Mer and chiefly in Côte des Huves les Éparges (near Verdun), on the front. On All Saints' Day in 1917 he sustained a serious head wound. For the rest of his life he suffered from the aftereffects of this wartime injury. Not until 1954 did an operation seem to mitigate de Lubac's condition appreciably, in that it relieved his constant bouts of dizziness and removed the threat of meningitis (*ASC*, p. 19).

It is typical of the fundamentally missionary inspiration of de Lubac's work that an intellectually open yet unbelieving comrade in arms whom he had befriended incited him to undertake his first literary activity. So as to have something to put into the hands of modern men like this friend, de Lubac wrote down some of his thoughts and collected from the great theological Tradition passages that transcended any dusty, antiquated experience of the Church and seemed to him suitable for opening the eyes of his enlightened contemporaries to the real meaning and beauty of faith in God and of life in the Church. Many years later, these notes would constitute the basis for the booklet *De la connaissance de Dieu*

(1945).[15] In it, de Lubac rejects all "psychological" interpretations of the concept of God and of its supposed development. The first two versions bore the dedication: "To my believing friends, and also to those who believe that they do not believe".

Philosophical Studies

After demobilization in 1919, de Lubac entered upon the education and formation that was customary for religious. He began by studying humanities at Saint Mary's College in Canterbury. Yet, instead of devoting himself intensively to the ancient languages, Latin and Greek, de Lubac, "intellectually starved" as a result of the war years, devoured Augustine's *Confessions*[16] and enthusiastically read the last three books of *Adversus haereses*, by Irenaeus of Lyons.[17] A no less important guide to his later studies was his reading of Pierre Rousselot's doctoral thesis on the *Intellectualisme de saint Thomas*, as well as the book-length article (250 columns!) on "Jésus-Christ" by Léonce de Grandmaison, S.J., in the *Dictionnaire apologétique* edited by d'Alès. Later on he would regret that he had not learned Greek better as he became increasingly aware of the preeminent importance of Origen; in order to read him he had to depend on Latin translations, particularly those by Rufinus of Aquileia.

[15] Henri de Lubac, *De la connaissance de Dieu* (1945), revised and reprinted as *Sur les chemins de Dieu* (1956). English edition: *The Discovery of God*, trans. Alexander Dru (New York: Kenedy & Sons, 1960; Grand Rapids, Mich.: Eerdmans, 1996). Citations here are from the 1996 edition. Cited as *DG*.

[16] St. Augustine, born 354 in North Africa, baptized 387, ordained a priest in 391, appointed Bishop of Hippo 396. He is a Doctor of the Church. His *Confessions* depict his meandering path to the Christian faith.

[17] St. Irenaeus of Lyons (died 202), Bishop of Lyons, came to grips with Gnosticism in five books entitled *Adversus haereses* (Against heresies). His was the first systematic presentation of the Christian faith.

De Lubac completed his three years of philosophy studies (1920–1923) in Jersey, England. During that time he enthusiastically read the works of Blondel together with his confrère Robert Hamel (d. 1974). This was possible only because some of his teachers disregarded the prohibition against Blondel's writings (on account of his suspected Modernism) in the Jesuit houses. In 1922, when de Lubac was sent by his superiors to the estate La Felicité not far from Aix to recover from an earache, he took the opportunity to visit the distinguished philosopher. A close friend of Blondel, Auguste Valensin,[18] with whom de Lubac had been acquainted since the time of his novitiate, arranged the meeting. De Lubac found his own impressions confirmed in an unpublished portrait of Blondel by Antoine Denat, which describes a visit to the philosopher in the year 1935:

> In his presence I understood from the outset what it meant to consider the teaching profession as a kind of priesthood. . . . In Maurice Blondel's patient voice and sustained eloquence there were at that time inflections of goodness, charity and urbanity, in the broad sense of that word, that I have rarely found in so developed and refined a degree in men of the Church. In the conversation of this so-called great "combatant" of ideas, there was not the least trace of . . . bitterness. . . . I left Maurice Blondel not only enlightened but calmed, and, reading his long works, which are more spoken than written, I found once again that immense patience, at once gentle and persistent, which ended in triumphing over all (quoted in *ASC*, p. 19).

[18] Auguste Valensin, S.J. (1879–1953), was professor of philosophy at the Catholic University of Lyons from 1920 on. He was a colleague, friend and, in the early years, a neighbor of de Lubac's and a friend of Teilhard de Chardin's and Blondel's. De Lubac published their correspondence: *Maurice Blondel et Auguste Valensin: Correspondance*, 3 vols. (1957 and 1965), and in *Textes et Documents Inédits* (1961).

Their first encounter was followed in 1938 by further visits, and even before that by a correspondence that documents the profound interior agreement of de Lubac with Blondel on the decisive question as to the supernatural tendency of created intellectual nature. In a letter dated April 3, 1932, de Lubac explicitly acknowledges that eleven years previously, as he was beginning to study philosophy, his reading of Blondel had inspired him to ponder the problem of *Surnaturel.*

A sentence from a letter written by Valensin to Blondel might illustrate the eminently important role that the philosopher played among the scholastics (that is, the Jesuit students there): "You are directing [!] the scholasticate in Ore from [your residence in] Aix. Day by day you are gaining influence. . . . That will make the Father General uneasy." [19]

After philosophy studies, Jesuit formation includes a period of practical activity in an institution of the Order. This is not only a time to make contact with people's living conditions and the working world, but also an opportunity to put to the test the skills and knowledge that the candidate has acquired thus far. At this point, de Lubac returned to the school in which he himself had encountered formative influences that would be important for his intellectual career: in the Jesuit College of Notre-Dame de Mongré, in Villefranche, he worked as the assistant to the prefect of studies.

As of 1924, the Jesuit students still had to go back to England for their subsequent studies in theology.

---

[19] Quoted in Albert Raffelt, "Maurice Blondel und die katholische Theologie in Deutschland", in Albert Raffelt et al., *Das Tun, Der Glaube, Die Vernunft: Studien zur Philosophie Maurice Blondels* (1995), p. 186.

Theological Studies

After the Jesuit schools were driven out of France, the theology students went at first to Canterbury. In 1907, however, the theologate was relocated to a new complex of buildings—Ore Place—that had been constructed on a hill overlooking Hastings. Only in 1926 was it possible to return the program to Lyons-Fourvière. And so de Lubac studied first for two years at Ore Place. In retrospect, he spoke gratefully of that time and praised the teachers he met there: "[A]nyone who did not live at Ore Place did not know in all its fullness the happiness of being a [Jesuit] scholastic. There we were really rather far from the world, away for a while from nearly all the responsibilities of the apostolate; alone among ourselves, as if in a big ship sailing, without a radio, in the middle of the ocean. But what an intense life within that ship, and what a marvelous crossing!" (*ASC*, p. 15). Along with Father Émile Delhaye, during that time Father Joseph Huby in particular trained the students "to explore in every sense [i.e., in all directions] the infinite spaces of dogmatics, to lose oneself, without getting lost, in the depths of mystery!" (ibid., p. 16). De Lubac read the classical works of theology, above all, Augustine, Bonaventure and, with particular diligence, Thomas Aquinas, the only author (besides the Evangelists) from whom he regularly copied out excerpts onto file cards during his student days (so that many of the teachers in Jersey called him a Thomist or a Neo-Thomist).

In his memoir *At the Service of the Church*, de Lubac mentions an especially productive and intellectually stimulating institution at Ore Place: the "free academies", an additional forum that went beyond the regular course of studies, in which topics could be chosen freely. There were three of these academies, and each student had to take part in one of them: one for pedagogy [education], one for social sciences and one for theology. De Lubac belonged to the theological academy, a group of ten students who regularly met on Sundays under the direction of Father Huby to discuss a selected topic on which one of the participants had prepared a talk. The framework of these academies gave de Lubac the opportunity to pursue the theme of the supernatural, which he had already recognized during his philosophy studies as being essential. Thus he composed during this time the first draft of the book that would appear in print in 1946 and subsequently would cause such a stir.

> [The subject] was at the center of the reflections of the masters about whom I have spoken: Rousselot, Blondel, Maréchal; we discovered it at the heart of all great Christian thought, whether that of Saint Augustine, Saint Thomas or Saint Bonaventure (for these were our classics par excellence); we noted that it was likewise at the bottom of the discussions with modern unbelief, that it formed the crux of the problem of Christian humanism. Father Huby, following the line of reflection inaugurated for us by Rousselot, had warmly urged me to verify whether the doctrine of Saint Thomas on this important point was indeed what was claimed by the Thomist school around the sixteenth century, codified in the seventeenth and asserted with greater emphasis than ever in the twentieth (ibid., p. 35).

Priestly Ordination and Year of Tertianship

In 1926, the climate in Church–State relations had improved to such an extent that the Jesuit college was able to return to France. De Lubac was ordained a priest on August 22, 1927. One year later, he had completed his theology studies in

Fourvière[20] and was then sent for his tertianship, the third year of probation, to Paray-le-Monial, where Father Auguste Bulot was his instructor. Without any preparation, de Lubac was appointed in September 1929 to succeed Father Albert Valensin in the chair of fundamental theology in the Faculty of Theology at the Catholic University of Lyons. Father Albert Valensin (1873–1944), the brother of Auguste Valensin, had not yet reached retirement age, but he asked to be relieved of his duties in order to devote himself entirely to ministry as a retreat master.

The Faculty of Theology at the Catholic University of Lyons (founded in 1875), of which de Lubac continued to be a member for the rest of his life, should be distinguished from the Jesuit preparatory school and college on the hill of Fourvière. The fact that de Lubac took up residence "above" in Fourvière, while continuing to teach as a professor "below", is confusing at first, and not only for outsiders: even many of de Lubac's superiors in Rome occasionally got mixed up about his assignment.

---

[20] Fourvière (from Latin *forum vetus*, "old forum") is the most ancient settlement of Lyons, site of Notre Dame Basilica (1872–1896), a landmark of the city and the destination of one of the most important Marian pilgrimages in France. From the mid-nineteenth century, it was also the location of a Jesuit preparatory school (*Collegium Maximum Lugdunense*), which in 1902 was outlawed and moved to England; the school returned in 1926 and was closed in 1974.

Professor in Lyons

Lyons is not only a place fraught with history, but also to this day, despite the separation of Church and State, a center of flourishing ecclesiastical life. The city is located at the confluence of the Saône and the Rhône rivers. The Romans settled on the hill overlooking the Saône. As the first Church founded in the West (after Rome) by the martyr-bishop Pothinus (d. A.D. 177), Lyons is the cradle of Christianity in France; it is important also as the scene of the ministry of his successor, the great Irenaeus (d. 202). On his feast day (June 28), the Catholic University of Lyons celebrates a liturgy at his tomb in the crypt of the Church of Saint Irenaeus. In the Middle Ages, Lyons hosted two councils: in 1245 (which, among other things, issued a decree about papal elections) and in 1274. Saint Thomas Aquinas died on his way to this second Council of Lyons. Presiding over it was Cardinal Bonaventure, who, shortly after bringing about a union with the Greeks (which was soon called off again), died of complete exhaustion on July 15, before the official conclusion of the Council, and was buried in Lyons.

After the storms of the French Revolution, Lyons recuperated spiritually, and its strong Christian atmosphere made it fertile soil for three missionary associations, which were started there in the first half of the nineteenth century. Beginning in 1892, Marius Gonin organized the *Semaines Sociales de France*, which since 1904 have addressed the challenges of an increasingly industrialized society, in keeping with the social Encyclical *Rerum novarum* (1891). Their mouthpiece is the publication *Chronique sociale* (founded in 1893), which is likewise headquartered in Lyons. In the assembly room of the *Chronique social*, de Lubac gave two lectures to a study group of Christian socialists, which would be incorporated into the first part of his book *Catholicisme* (*ASC*, p. 27). In them he opposed all interpretations of Christianity that limit the Good News to a message of individualistic salvation and defended the thesis that Catholicism is by its very essence social, so much so that the expression "social Catholicism" is unnecessarily redundant (*Cath*, p. 15).

In Lyons in 1930, de Lubac made the acquaintance of an eminent expert in Far Eastern religions (who read texts in the original Sanskrit), the Abbé Monchanin, who would introduce him to the world of Buddhism. Monchanin himself went to India in 1939 as a missionary. From 1950 on, he lived a life completely devoted to contemplation and returned to France only in 1957 as he was dying. De Lubac erected a monument for him in 1967: a small, lovingly prepared volume with a lively narrative and illustrated with several photographs. The little book,[1] which is dedicated to the priests of the Archdiocese of Lyons, not only portrays this impressive priest and missionary but also gives the reader a vivid glimpse of the intellectual and ecclesiastical life of Lyons in the 1930s. Chapter Three (pp. 29–37), for example, is devoted to the Abbé Couturier, who had become acquainted in Belgium with the Octave of Prayer for Christian Unity and introduced it in Lyons in 1933. Through the Abbé Couturier, de Lubac

---

[1] Henri de Lubac, *Images de l'abbé Monchanin* (1967). This little volume won the 1968 *Grand prix catholique de littérature* [first-place award for Catholic literature].

became involved in the ecumenical movement. Once he was invited to preach during the Octave of Prayer. This brought him into contact with the two young Swiss ministers, Roger Schutz and Max Thurian, who in the 1940s founded the evangelical monastic community of Taizé near Cluny, not far from Lyons (*ASC*, p. 45).

My Sole Passion

In September of 1929, de Lubac moved for the time being "downhill" to the Jesuit house on the Rue d'Auvergne (an old, ramshackle building, as he himself notes). In October 1929 the new instructor gave his inaugural lecture, "Apologetics and Theology".[2] In it, de Lubac outlines a form of apologetics (defense of the faith) that is different from the usual view of this theological subject that he is about to teach. In the Neo-Scholastic course of studies, it was considered the task of apologetics to defend the self-contained and fixed doctrinal system of Catholic beliefs (as it is comprehensively set forth in dogmatic theology) against the objections of religious critics and to safeguard it from the questions and challenges that arose during the Reformation. De Lubac never disputed the importance of a sound "defense of the faith", which is always a sign of its vitality as well. In fact, in a 1961 letter to the Vicar General of the Society of Jesus he wrote, "The sole passion of my life is the defense of our faith" (*ASC*, p. 324). Still, in his book *Catholicism: Christ and the Common Destiny of Man*, he complains somewhat that it is a great misfortune to have learned the catechism *against* someone (*Cath*, 309). When one is on the defensive, one is always weak, allowing the opponent to choose the topics; one

---

[2] Henri de Lubac, "Apologétique et théologie", published as an essay in *Nouvelle revue théologique* in 1930.

remains dependent upon criticism and runs the risk of losing sight of the genuine strength and beauty of one's own position and of obscuring it in the sight of others. Never, de Lubac says, should the Church content herself with the mere proof that she is still alive. Rather, she is sent to go forth into the world and to bring the Gospel to everyone. Therefore de Lubac—clearly inspired by Maurice Blondel—endeavors to make allowances for the intellectual situation of modern man, who is to a great extent alienated from the faith and the Church. He prefers not to regard the faith of the Church as a self-contained block, which originates in a divine decree and which man must therefore accept without any explanation as to what it all has to do with his life. Taking as its point of departure man, as a being that is ordered to the divine transcendence, the kind of apologetics that Henri de Lubac has in mind should demonstrate how the Gospel message addresses the real questions of the human spirit and should finally (to use an expression of Augustine) prove to the pagans, through reason, how unreasonable it is not to believe. In this process, the path from reason to faith is by no means a one-way street. After "insight into the faith" comes "insight through the faith". The light of faith illuminates reason and makes possible an ever-deeper knowledge of the mystery of God and of man. De Lubac's inaugural lecture in 1929 marked a turning point in the history of theology from apologetics to fundamental theology as it is widely understood today.

Again and again Henri de Lubac deplored the fact that he had not been prepared for his new assignment as seminary instructor. He had not been required to write a doctoral thesis (the degree was necessary, and so it had been conferred upon him *pro forma*), and whenever he requested time for study later on, his petition was always denied. Instead he received an additional teaching assignment. As early as the spring of 1930, the dean of the faculty, Podechard, asked him to prepare to give lectures in the history of religion, too. In 1938, he was appointed professor of fundamental theology, and finally, in 1939, he was made a professor for the history of religion, as well.

In Lyons Henri de Lubac instructed theology students from forty different dioceses and members of many religious communities, yet not one single Jesuit student; furthermore, he himself was the sole Jesuit among the professors on the theology faculty [at the Catholic University]. His friend, confrere and housemate Auguste Valensin was an instructor on the philosophy faculty.

Prominent among de Lubac's colleagues on the theology faculty were the two deans, the first being Emmanuel Podechard, a Sulpician Father and Old Testament scholar. Work in this field was still greatly impeded in the 1930s by the restrictions of the Pontifical Bible Commission, which caused Podechard, an obedient man of the Church, much suffering, since he could not publish the results of his research. Later on, Georges Jouassard, a patrologist who also taught the history of doctrine, became de Lubac's dean. Jouassard, a man who had a knack for diplomacy, observed already in the thirties with some uneasiness how candidly de Lubac presented his theology, which collided with many Neo-Scholastic positions, and he warned him of the possible consequences. Later, however, after the outbreak of the anticipated conflict, he stood by him and, as de Lubac emphasizes, became more and more of a friend to him.

Fourvière: The Myth and the Reality

The fact that Henri de Lubac moved in 1934 to take up residence in the Jesuit college in Lyons-Fourvière "up on the hill" was to have extremely important consequences for the history of theology. Although he had nothing to do with the program of studies at the Jesuit scholasticate (with the exception of a few lectures on Buddhism and a brief period of substituting for a dogmatic theologian who fell ill), he would make an influential impression on a whole generation of young Jesuit students who studied in Fourvière in the thirties and forties but were only bored, not to mention repulsed, by the Scholastic theology that was offered there, while they were fascinated by Henri de Lubac, who lived in the same house. Hans Urs von Balthasar recalls that

> Fortunately Henri de Lubac was in residence, and he referred us beyond scholasticism to the Church Fathers, generously making his notes and excerpts available to us. So it came about that while others were playing soccer, I studied with Daniélou, Bouillard and a number of others (Fessard was no longer there), and I wrote books about Origen, Gregory of Nyssa, and Maximus.[3]

A vivid picture is provided also by the memoirs of another student at Fourvière at that time, Xavier Tilliette (b. 1921), who writes that de Lubac

> was not an instructor in the scholasticate, but rather "below" on the Catholic University faculty. Despite his exhaustion he never returned with the *funiculaire*, but rather climbed laboriously back up by way of the narrow, steep streets. "Above", nevertheless, he conducted a sort of clandestine teaching ministry; professors and students both visited his room regularly. He himself was never concerned about having "disciples"—"One is your Master"—but rather about

---

[3] Hans Urs von Balthasar, *Test Everything, Keep What Is Good* (San Francisco: Ignatius Press, 1986), pp. 11–12.

inspiring them to be diligent theologians. Their studies were
supposed to give form to their existence and train them to be
witnesses to Christ. Out of this quiet, unpretentious course
of instruction grew what one might call the "Fourvière
school". But who will depict this theological springtime,
which flourished there shortly before and during the horrible
war years? Basically it was not a "school" at all, much less
a "new theology". Instead, the old patristic sources, which
were close to early Christianity, began to bubble up again
and poured forth in many streams. . . . The schoolmaster was
a suffering man who had brought back home from the First
World War a serious head injury that impeded his work for
days and weeks on end. Quite often we found him in an easy
chair or stretched out on his bed, scarcely able to speak. We
devoured his books. . . . From one single central vision his
work developed in every direction, just as a free-standing
tree spreads out its branches. He attached great importance
to the "conversion of heart" required at the beginning of
theological study. He insisted on objectivity, submission to
the *datum*, that is, to what is given, and when this is Divine
Revelation, then submission to the mystery.[4]

This group of young, gifted theologians gathered around
their friend and master, Henri de Lubac, had such vitality and
innovative theological power that opponents later spoke of a
"Fourvière school" and the whole thing even ballooned into
a "myth of Fourvière".

Sources chrétiennes and Théologie

The productivity of this young generation of theologians was
manifested in two series of publications. Henri de Lubac
played an influential part in both of them.

[4] Xavier Tilliette, "Henri de Lubac achtzigjährig", *Internationale Katholische
Zeitschrift Communion* 5 (1976): 187, n. 12.

The idea for the series *Sources chrétiennes* (literally: Christian Sources) goes back to the time before the Second World War. The project was the brainchild of Father Victor Fontoynont,[5] who initially had in mind the publication of texts by the Greek Church Fathers only, which he thought would be a promising resource in the ecumenical encounter with the Eastern Churches. With the beginning of the war and the transfer of Father Chaillet, who was in charge of the project at first, responsibility for it fell to Henri de Lubac. In 1942, the first volume appeared: a translation of Gregory of Nyssa's *Life of Moses*, by Jean Daniélou.[6] De Lubac and Daniélou worked together as editors of the series: Daniélou, in Paris, was responsible for advertising and distribution in occupied France, while de Lubac in Lyons did the same for unoccupied France. Experts in their respective fields were recruited to present unabridged texts of the Latin and Greek Church Fathers, and the writings of medieval theologians as well. After the war, the volumes took on an increasingly scholarly character. Besides the French translation, most volumes presented a critical edition of the original text, along with historical and theological introductions. The series *Sources chrétiennes*, which by 1999 had grown to more than 440 volumes, not only made possible a remarkable renewal in the study of patristics, which has had a lasting influence on French theology and the spirituality of the French Church, but it also set editorial standards and served as an example for the German-speaking world (since 1990 the series *Fontes*

---

[5] Victor Fontoynont, S.J. (1880–1958), was former prefect of studies for the theologate in Lyons-Fourvière.

[6] Jean Daniélou, S.J. (1905–1974), was a student and friend of de Lubac's. In 1943, he was appointed professor for early Christian literature and history at the Institut Catholique in Paris. He co-founded the series *Sources chrétiennes* and collaborated in the Second Vatican Council. In 1969, he was created a cardinal.

Christiani—Latin for "Christian sources"—has been published by Herder).

The publishers of *Sources chrétiennes* realized that it is not enough simply to make the texts available and to repeat the slogan "back to the sources". Also needed is an explication of the enduring content of patristic theology and its application to a different set of contemporary issues.

Another series was dedicated to this purpose of supplementing the collection of sources through the publication of special studies of themes in patristic and medieval theology. This second collection was called *Théologie*, with the subtitle "Studies published under the direction of the Theology Faculty of the Society of Jesus in Lyons-Fourvière". The publishing house Aubier in Paris began to print this series, too, even before the end of the Second World War. Volume 1 was the Roman dissertation of Henri Bouillard[7] on *Conversion and Grace in Thomas Aquinas* (1944), in which he, citing Rousselot and other [twentieth-century] theologians, set out along the path of reconstructing what Saint Thomas really meant. Jean Daniélou's doctoral dissertation on Gregory of Nyssa was printed as volume 2. Volume 3, which appeared in 1944, was *Corpus mysticum*, by Henri de Lubac, who subsequently was to publish most of his monographs in this series.

His First: "An Outstanding Book"

Besides his teaching duties at the university, de Lubac was invited to give lectures on various subjects. This resulted in

[7] Henri Bouillard, S.J. (1908–1981), was a professor of dogmatic theology in Lyons-Fourvière and the first editor-in-chief of the series *Théologie*. In 1950, he, de Lubac and others were recalled from Lyons because of suspicions that they were teaching a "new theology". In 1957, he took a degree at a state university in Paris with his dissertation on Karl Barth. In 1967, he joined the faculty of the Institut catholique in Paris.

several essays, some of which were published. When Father
Yves Congar, O.P.,[8] asked de Lubac for a volume on an
ecclesiological theme for the series *Unam Sanctam*, which
Congar edited, he suggested that de Lubac compile a collection of these essays as a book. That was the origin of de
Lubac's first book, *Catholicisme: Les aspects sociaux du dogme*
[*Catholicism: Christ and the Common Destiny of Man*], which
first appeared in 1938 and was reprinted many times. From
the chapters of this book came "the branches of the subsequent major works as though from a single trunk", as Hans
Urs von Balthasar has incisively noted. Therefore the book is
a good introduction to reading de Lubac, but also a suitable
companion to the later major works. For in these short early
essays we often find the later theses and main arguments in a
form that is concentrated and easy to grasp. A comparison
between *Catholicisme* and the later works shows, moreover,
the great consistency of de Lubac's thought, with no breaks or
discrepancies whatsoever. As early as 1943, Hans Urs von
Balthasar's German translation of *Catholicisme* was published
by Benziger, and a second edition was printed in 1970 by
Balthasar's own publishing house, Johannes Verlag. Balthasar's
struggle to find an exact German rendering of the title
illustrates the questions that arose as to the essential theme
of the book. The first edition was called *Katholizismus als
Gemeinschaft* [Catholicism as Community], which closely resembles the original French title. But that wasn't quite right,
as Balthasar himself later realized (see p. 23, n. 9). In all the
essays of this book, de Lubac is not concerned with present-

[8] Yves Congar, O.P. (1904–1995), was appointed a professor of dogmatic
theology at the scholasticate of the Dominican Order in Le Saulchoir in 1931.
From 1956 to 1968, he taught in Strasbourg, and from then on, in Paris.
Together with de Lubac, he was appointed in 1960 to the theological commission that prepared the Second Vatican Council. He was created a cardinal in
1994.

ing what is specifically Catholic as a "denomination". The reader expecting such a book would find that both a chapter on the papacy and reflections on the importance of Tradition were missing. Yet de Lubac by no means intended to produce a Catholic manual on the Church. He is concerned, rather, about catholicity as a dimension of the Church. From the first moment of her existence, the Church has been catholic, inasmuch as "in each individual [she] calls on the whole man, embracing him as he is in his whole nature" (*Cath*, p. 49).

Karl Rahner, who reviewed the book in the *Zeitschrift für Katholische Theologie*, hit the nail on the head:

> An outstanding book. Although written in a simple, clear style for a wider readership, about questions that are "timely", it nevertheless has considerable theological depth. It does not deal with that part of the Church's moral doctrine which is called her social teaching, nor with "labor union" questions, but rather with the unity of all mankind in Christ and in the Church. It explains the insight that, according to the most essential tenets of the Christian faith, mankind is not merely an external, incidental sum of single individuals, each of which is working for his own salvation. Mankind, rather—in the original soteriological plan, in the Fall, in its redemption by Christ, in all of salvation history from Adam to the end of the world and even in eternal salvation—is a holy unity in Christ and in the Church.[9]

Corpus mysticum

Before the war, de Lubac had written a book—*Corpus mysticum*—that could not be published until 1944. He had been appointed the second examiner for the defense of a doctoral dissertation on Archdeacon Florius of Lyons (ninth century),

---

[9] Karl Rahner, review of *Catholicisme, Zeitschrift für Katholische Theologie* 63 (1939): 443f., reprinted in K. Rahner, *Sämtliche Werke*, vol. 4 (1997), pp. 484f.

and so he had to read up on the history of the theology of the Eucharist. While on vacation in Aix-en-Provence to recuperate, he made use of the opportunity, not only to meet several times with the revered Maurice Blondel, but also to study the relationship between Eucharist and Church. Without any preconceived ideas from secondary literature, de Lubac immersed himself in a study of the sources and made an interesting discovery with regard to the definition of the Church as *Corpus Christi* (the Body of Christ), as Paul called the Church. During the course of the first millennium, more specific nuances were added to the idea of Corpus Christi. The True Body of Christ, Corpus Christi *verum*, is the Church, while Corpus Christi *mysticum* is the Eucharist. In the early medieval period there was a stronger emphasis on the Real Presence of Christ in the Eucharist, and the adjectives were switched. Now the Eucharistic Body of Christ is the Corpus Christi *verum*, while the Church became the Corpus Christi *mysticum*. In the book he titled *Corpus mysticum*[10], de Lubac shows how in the following centuries the Church as a mystery of faith disappears little by little from Christian consciousness.[11] This rediscovery of the sacramental concept of the Church decisively prepared the way for the understanding of the Church that was formulated by the Second Vatican Council, which, in article 1 of *Lumen gentium*, says: "[T]he Church, in Christ, is in the nature of a sacrament—a sign and an instrument, that is, of communion with God and of unity among all men."

[10] Henri de Lubac, *Corpus mysticum: L'Eucharistie et l'Église au Moyen Âge*, Étude historique (Paris: Aubier, 1944).
[11] On this subject, see below, pp. 179–81.

World War II and Intellectual Resistance

On May 10, 1940, the German Army suddenly invaded France. War and occupation forced de Lubac to flee from Lyons twice. Despite internal and external tribulations, it was a creative and productive time. His intellectual grappling with the ideologies of National Socialism and Marxism resulted in writings that have validity well beyond the occasions for their composition.

After the occupation of Paris on June 14, 1940, France was conquered. Marshal Pétain (1856–1951), who had made a reputation for himself during the First World War by his successful defense of Verdun and who had held various political offices since that war, was elected premier (or prime minister) by the Parliament on June 16. He negotiated the cease-fire with Hitler in Compiègne on June 22. France was divided into an occupied Northern Zone and a free Southern Zone. On July 11, Pétain was made chief of state also. The headquarters of the Vichy Government were located at the health resort Vichy in the Massif Central. Pétain cooperated in a limited way with the occupying power and proclaimed laws along National-Socialist lines with regard to the Jewish population. Parallel to the Vichy government, a Provisional National Committee of Free Frenchmen was established in London under the leadership of General de Gaulle. Until the Southern Zone was likewise occupied, Lyons was the center of Free France and thus also the center of the intellectual and political resistance.

Manuscripts in His Luggage

In June 1940, de Lubac, together with a group of colleagues, left Lyons for the first time to set out for La Louvesc (located south of Lyons, in the Massif Central), so as to escape the advancing German troops. In his luggage, he carried the materials that he had meanwhile collected for the book *Surnaturel*. At the safe location he put the excerpts in order, and the book began to take shape. According to de Lubac's memoirs, it was ready for publication as early as 1941.

After the capitulation of France and its division, the line of demarcation was drawn north of Lyons, and so de Lubac returned to Lyons, and the scholasticate was at first able to continue in operation as usual. During the 1941–1942 academic year, de Lubac gave lectures on the early French socialist Pierre Joseph Proudhon (1809–1865). Soon after the war's end, it was possible to publish them as a book.[1]

Proudhon, who quarreled furiously with Karl Marx in 1848 and finally broke with him, fascinated de Lubac as a seeker who, although outwardly traveling other paths and fighting against the Church, nevertheless, for the rest of his life, could not rid himself of the idea of God.

The book about Proudhon, which was based on a wide range of previously unknown or at least unpublished letters and other documents, has not been surpassed as an evaluation of the source materials and is still the necessary point of departure for further studies on the subject of Proudhon and Christianity.

---

[1] Henri de Lubac, *Proudhon et le christianisme* (1945). English edition: *The Un-Marxian Socialist: A Study of Proudhon*, trans. R. E. Scantlebury (New York: Sheed & Ward, 1948).

War Reaches Lyons

De Lubac expressly denied that he was repeatedly arrested by the Germans, as has been sometimes reported. It is true, however, that after the German troops had marched into the hitherto free zone, including Lyons, in the fall of 1942, he had to flee the city again in 1943, because the Gestapo were looking for him. This time he found refuge in a religious house in Vals (a spa south of Lyons). He used this time of complete seclusion to rework and expand his book *Surnaturel*. "Taking advantage of the resources offered by the Vals library, the manuscript swelled. When I came back to Lyons soon after the departure of the German army, it was ready to be delivered to the printer" (*ASC*, p. 35).

Yet a third book originated during the war years and clearly shows traces of his intellectual resistance against totalitarianism: *Le drame de l'humanisme athée* (*The Drama of Atheist Humanism*), 1944, which, like *Catholicism*, is a work made up of essays that had at first been written independently of one another. The first part consists of a series of semi-clandestine lectures along anti-Nazi lines, while the second, more homogeneous, part is his lecture on Auguste Comte and that writer's concept of "positive religion"; the third part is a collection of several "ardent but, I must admit, rather superficial" essays on Dostoyevsky (*ASC*, p. 40). The first German translation by Eberhard Steinacker (*Die Tragödie des Humanismus ohne Gott* [1950], now out of print) was superseded by the revised 1984 German version of Hans Urs von Balthasar.[2]

---

[2] Henri de Lubac, *Le Drame de l'humanisme athée* (1944); *Über Gott hinaus: Tragödie des atheistischen Humanismus*, rev. trans. by Hans Urs von Balthasar (1984). English editions: *The Drama of Atheist Humanism*, trans. Edith M. Riley (New York: Sheed & Ward, 1950); trans. Albert Wimmer (San Francisco: Ignatius Press, 1995). The 1995 edition is cited here as *DAH*.

The latter, like the 1983 revised and enlarged French edition, includes as an appendix another essay on the theme of "Nietzsche as Mystic", which de Lubac had published in 1950 in the anthology *Affrontements mystiques*. This essay is, as von Balthasar says, "also important for our modern understanding of Nietzsche since, with his characteristic lucidity, Henri de Lubac attempts to solve the psychological riddle of Nietzsche's efforts to overcome or sustain the contradiction between the 'Overman' and 'Eternal Return'" (*DAH*, p. 10). The fundamental idea of the individual essays is the downright tragic misunderstanding of modern humanism, which pits God and man against one another and proceeds from the assumption that dependence upon God demeans man and destroys his freedom, so that man can attain his true greatness only if he renounces the idea of God. In another passage, de Lubac states the theme quite concisely: "God is rejected as limiting man—and people forget that it is man's relation to God that confers upon him 'a sort of infinity.' God is rejected as enslaving man—and people forget that it is man's relation to God that frees him from all servitudes. . . . Man without God is dehumanized" (*DG*, p. 194, 193).

Intellectual Resistance—*Les Cahiers du Témoignage chrétien*

With the book *Résistance chrétienne à l'antisémitisme* (1988),[3] de Lubac intended to snatch from oblivion the manifold initiatives that Christians took against the persecution of the Jews and to protect those efforts from false interpretations. While he was far from justifying the stance of all the bishops with

[3] Henri de Lubac, *Christian Resistance to Anti-Semitism: Memories from 1940– 1944*, trans. Elizabeth Englund (San Francisco: Ignatius Press, 1990). Cited as *CR*.

regard to the Vichy government, de Lubac categorically denied that he was the author of a memoir attributed to him in
the years immediately after the war that was highly critical of
the French episcopate.[4] De Lubac expressly wanted his sort of
resistance against Nazism to be understood as *intellectual* and
not political resistance. This was all the more imperative for
him, since the political stance of many a superior was not
exactly unambiguous.

In October 1940 the Vichy government promulgated its
first laws concerning the Jews (which would be made even
more restrictive through other measures, in particular those
passed on June 2, 1941). All Jews in France were obliged to
register and to wear the Star of David in public: these were
preliminary measures leading up to deportation and mass
murder. Among converts to Christianity, a distinction was
made between those who were baptized before June 25, 1940,
and those who received baptism after that date. In French
cinema theaters, the Nazi propaganda film *Jud Süss* was
shown. In a confidential memorandum to one of his religious
superiors, dated April 25, 1941, de Lubac expresses his shock
at the vile and inhumane procedures whereby anti-Semitism
was attempting to gain adherents in France.[5] He recalls the
decisive rejection of any form of anti-Semitism whatsoever
by the Church's Magisterium; he criticizes the legislation and
warns against the intrusion of this malign spirit even into
religious houses. The memorandum was well received by his
superiors, but not by Father Norbert Boynes, S.J., the Assistant General, who visited France in the period 1940–1942

---

[4] Jacques Prévotat, "Les Évêques sous l'Occupation: un démenti du cardinal de Lubac", *Communio* (French edition), 17 (1992): 126–32.

[5] Henri de Lubac's memorandum against anti-Semitism was published in its
entirety in Jean Chelini, *L'Église sous Pie XII: la Tourmente, 1939–1945* (1983),
pp. 295–310. Excerpts were printed also in *CR*, p. 251.

and objected to the lack of loyalty to the Vichy regime on the part of many younger Jesuits. De Lubac, who was one of those targeted by these accusations, wrote a passionate letter in self-defense to his Provincial Superior (July 24, 1941), in which he put up a fight against the attempts to "throw [him] out of the Society of Jesus permanently, so to speak", without stating the grounds for the charges. He insists repeatedly that he had never violated the two principles that ought to regulate the conduct of Jesuits in political questions: (1) Jesuits are not supposed to be involved in politics but rather must work for the Kingdom of God. (2) Requisite loyalty to the government should be distinguished from one's stance with regard to its legislation, about which a theologian may venture to pass judgment, especially at a time when the practice of religion is so seriously endangered (see *ASC*, 245–46).

We should note in this connection, besides the previously mentioned essays that were collected in *The Drama of Atheist Humanism*, de Lubac's participation in the project entitled *Cahiers du Témoignage chrétien* (the Christian Witness series), which was spearheaded by Father Pierre Chaillet, S.J. In the fall of 1941, the first volume appeared. It bore the title *France, prends garde de perdre ton âme* (France, beware, lest you lose your soul) and had been written entirely by Father Gaston Fessard, S.J. Other volumes then appeared in quick succession. De Lubac not only wrote for the series (anonymously, so that authorship of particular contributions can no longer be determined, but also carefully reviewed each one of the volumes and even read the galley proofs. They were supposed to maintain a high scholarly standard while at the same time manifesting complete loyalty to the Catholic Church.

The Archbishop of Paris, Cardinal Jean-Marie Lustiger, recalls that he observed the fortieth anniversary of the libera-

tion of Paris (1944) by celebrating a Mass of Thanksgiving at
Notre Dame Cathedral in Paris in August of 1984:

> On that day, I had the grace to have Cardinal de Lubac beside
> me, and I was able to quote some of his articles that in
> wartime had appeared in the underground journal *Témoign-*
> *age chrétien* and that do great honor to the Church. These
> spiritual and theological texts were also political, in the
> strongest sense of the word; they spoke of respect for man
> and its idolatrous negation. The very fact that, forty years
> later, Cardinal de Lubac and I were concelebrating that Mass
> in the cathedral of Notre-Dame de Paris in the presence of
> government officials meant that a judgment was being passed
> on that period—and to me that seemed very important.[6]

In one issue of the *Témoignage chrétien*, the editors published
the following text by the Bishop of Berlin, Count Konrad
von Preysing,[7] who, during the time of the Third Reich, had
been one of the courageous Church leaders who stood on the
front lines in the Church's spiritual battle against the National-Socialist regime in Germany.

> No doubt is possible for us: we are Christians, engaged in a
> hard battle. Against us is rising the religion of blood. The
> signs of the fight are flashing everywhere, everywhere from
> the scornful rejection of the doctrine of Christ to impas-
> sioned and overt hatred. A drumroll of claims [barrage of
> allegations] borrowed both from history and from the present
> is surging over us. The goal of the battle is clear: it is the
> suppression and expulsion of Christianity. A joyful clamor of

[6] See Jean-Marie Lustiger, *Choosing God, Chosen by God* (San Francisco:
Ignatius Press, 1991), pp. 89–90. Lustiger, who was born Jewish in 1926, was
baptized on August 25, 1940, after taking instructions from Bishop Courcoux
of Orléans. In 1979, he himself was made Bishop of Orléans; and in 1980,
Archbishop of Paris. In 1983 (together with de Lubac), he was created a
cardinal. Lustiger's mother was murdered in 1943 in Auschwitz.

[7] Konrad von Preysing (1880–1950) became Bishop of Eichstätt in 1932,
Bishop of Berlin in 1935; and he was created a cardinal in 1946.

victory is rising from the ranks of anti-Christianity (*ASC*, pp. 51–52).

Two years after the end of the war, on Saturday, August 30, 1947, de Lubac met in Berlin with Bishop Konrad von Preysing: "When, in 1947, in Berlin, I had a conversation with Msgr. von Preysing, we embraced with emotion, stating that, from both sides, we had led the same combat, against the same adversary of Christ, with the same spiritual weapons" (*ASC*, p. 51). According to Herbert Vorgrimler,[8] de Lubac considered his meeting with Bishop von Preysing and their exchange on the subject of the *Résistance* as one of "the most important outward events of his life".

After the war von Preysing was the bishop of a divided city, the Eastern half of which had been freed from one totalitarian regime only to fall under the dominion of another. In a pastoral letter from the year 1949 on the relation of modern man to God, he quoted almost word for word de Lubac's analyses from *The Drama of Atheist Humanism*. "For more than a hundred years, the modern world has dreamed and talked about a complete emancipation of man. It was believed that the idea of God was the obstacle for man's free development, that the liberation of man was not possible without his liberation from God. We are standing in the presence of the ruins that the emancipation of man has brought about. Visible, tangible ruins, but even more painfully: spiritual ruins."[9]

The dark clouds of war had scarcely dispersed when suspicions about de Lubac's orthodoxy resurfaced. The storm broke in the year 1946.

---

[8] Herbert Vorgrimler, "Henri de Lubac", in Hans Jürgen Schultz, ed., *Tendenzen der Theologie im 20. Jahrhundert: Eine Geschichte in Portraits* [Trends in twentieth-century theology: a history in biographical sketches] (1966), p. 419.

[9] Quoted from Stephan Adam, *Bischof Konrad von Preysing* (1996), pp. 190f., n. 812.

A "New Theology"?

De Lubac speaks of fifteen sorrowful years that followed almost immediately after the time of the German occupation. In his memoir, *At the Service of the Church*, he writes unsparingly about the conduct of his opponents and the weakness of many of his superiors. Even though in these lines he expresses his pain over so much injustice, mediocrity and lack of charity, his words are nevertheless free of bitterness. De Lubac's rejection of all later attempts to misuse his case as an occasion for criticism directed at "Rome" and ecclesiastical structures of authority is more harshly worded than his judgment on those who did him an injustice.

Le Surnaturel

Ever since the days when he was studying philosophy, de Lubac had researched the question of the final destination of man and the ultimate purpose of human nature. Inspired by the philosophy of Maurice Blondel and encouraged by Father Joseph Huby, he traced this inquiry through the individual stages in the history of theology and was compelled to conclude that in the sixteenth and seventeenth centuries a change had come about in Catholic theology.

De Lubac had already published these insights of his to some extent in individual essays. During the wartime months in which he had to flee from Lyons, he continued his work on this subject also, so that by 1942 a first draft of the book, with the simple title *Surnaturel* (The Supernatural) and the subtitle *Études historiques* (Historical Studies), was ready for publication. Additional weeks of leisure allowed the work to be expanded further, until finally, in the fall of 1945, it was able to go to press so as to appear in the spring of 1946. Although de Lubac explicitly countered the objection that in his book he was questioning the gratuitous character of grace as a gift, this was precisely the main objection that would be leveled against him.[1]

Surnaturel was not the only reason for the campaign that now began, and de Lubac was not the only theologian who found himself under attack. Still, the publication of his study was one of the more important catalysts, and Henri de Lubac was perhaps the most prominent and articulate theologian in a movement that others now tried to label *la nouvelle théologie*—the "New Theology".

A Remake of Modernism?

Nouvelle théologie is a battle cry. De Lubac, at least, never used it to describe his own thought. In a letter to Hubert Schnackers, who in the 1970s wrote a doctoral dissertation on de Lubac's understanding of the Church,[2] he wrote:

> I do not much like it when people talk of a "new theology", referring to me; I have never used the expression, and I detest the thing. I have always sought, on the contrary, to make the Tradition of the Church known, in what it offers that is most universal and least subject to the variations of time. "New theology" is a polemical term, . . . which most of the time signifies nothing, serving only to throw suspicion on the

[1] See below, pp. 122–38.
[2] Hubert Schnackers, *Die Kirche als Sakrament und Mutter* (1979).

author in the mind of those who do not take a closer look at it (unless some today, on the contrary, take pride in it) (quoted from *ASC*, p. 361).

Not only does de Lubac not consider his own theology "a new theology"; on the contrary, he is able to describe as a "New Theology" precisely that theory of a *natura pura* which he so vehemently disputed (see *Surnaturel*, p. 140). Therefore this expression should not be applied to characterize de Lubac's theology.

The expression had already been coined at the time of the Modernist crisis, but from 1942 on it has increasingly been in vogue.

In 1946, the esteemed Father Garrigou-Lagrange, O.P.[3] (who was Karol Wojtyła's doctoral dissertation advisor), published in the journal *Angelicum* an essay entitled *"La théologie nouvelle: où va-t-elle?"*, in which he posed the question "Where is the New Theology headed?", which he immediately answered in no uncertain terms: "It leads to Modernism!" With that, the weapon was definitively forged.

In August 1946, the General Congregation of the Jesuits convened in Rome to elect a new General for the Order (because of wartime disturbances it had not been possible to elect a successor immediately after the death of Father Ledochowski on December 13, 1942). Henri de Lubac was the delegate from his Jesuit Province and stayed in Rome from August until October 28, 1946. On September 15, Father Jean-Baptiste Janssens (1889–1964, a Belgian, was elected General Superior.

Two days later, the Pope received the delegates to the General Assembly in an audience at Castel Gandolfo and gave a speech in which, among other things, he expressed criticism

---

[3] Dominican friars put the abbreviation O.P. after their names; it stands for *Ordo Praedicatorum*—the Order of Preachers.

of the fact that on several occasions lately there had been excessively imprudent talk of "New Theology". After the *allocutio*, the Jesuit Fathers were introduced to the Pope individually, and each one exchanged a few words with him. Pius XII said to de Lubac in a friendly tone of voice, "Ah! I know your doctrine very well!" De Lubac therefore saw no reason to be uneasy. But then the Pope's speech was unexpectedly printed two days later in *L'Osservatore Romano*. Instantly the rumors and suspicions proliferated as to whom could be meant, to which doctrinal objections this criticism might have been alluding, and what the disciplinary consequences might be. De Lubac published his diary entries for the period from September 9, 1946, to April 18, 1947, as an appendix to his book *At the Service of the Church* [4:4, pp. 250–57]. Catastrophic prognostications were making the rounds, going so far as to imply a supposedly impending condemnation of the "School of Fourvière". Yet everything was still vague. No superior mentioned any concrete accusations against de Lubac, so that he might express his views on the subject. Alfredo Ottaviani,[4] whom he visited on October 1 in the Sacrum Officium, reassured him that the Pope's address was not meant to discourage him in his work.

We can surmise that political motives played a part, too, in the affair that was now under way, since it is possible to connect the dots between the Vichy government and the rejection of the *Nouvelle théologie*. At any rate, some of the driving forces among de Lubac's opponents were the same men who had accused him of disloyalty toward Marshal

---

[4] Alfredo Ottaviani (1890–1979) was appointed an *assessor* of the *Sacrum Officium* (the "Holy Office", now called the Congregation for the Doctrine of the Faith); was created a cardinal in 1953; served as Prefect of the *Sacrum Officium* from 1959 to 1968 and as chairman of the Theological Preparatory Commission for the Second Vatican Council in 1959.

Pétain during the Occupation. Father Garrigou-Lagrange had gone so far in his defense of Pétain as to characterize any form of support for de Gaulle as mortally sinful.[5]

Outwardly, everything was still calm, but the stone had started to roll. Taking the lead publicly as opponents of de Lubac were Father Garrigou-Lagrange, O.P., a professor at the Pontifical University of Saint Thomas Aquinas (the Angelicum) and Father Charles Boyer, S.J., along with a few other confreres of de Lubac from the Society of Jesus, who tried with all their might to influence the new General and to force him to issue a condemnation of what they called the "New Theology". De Lubac was confident—at least to begin with—that he had Father Janssens' support and continued his work unperturbed.

A Peaceable Book in Stormy Times

While all around him extremely turbulent storms were beginning to break, de Lubac somehow found the interior peace in which to prepare one of his most important books: *Histoire et Esprit* (1950).[6]

For twenty years already de Lubac had been researching Origen (A.D. 185–254) and his theology. Little by little he became aware of the outstanding importance of this man, who suffered so much injustice from posterity and to this day remains one of the most controversial theologians in all of history.

---

[5] Martin Lenk, *Von der Gotteserkenntnis: Natürliche Theologie im Werk Henri de Lubacs* [On the knowledge of God: natural theology in the writings of Henri de Lubac] (1993).

[6] Henri de Lubac, English translation: *History and Spirit: The Understanding of Scripture according to Origen* (San Francisco: Ignatius Press, 2007); cited as *HS*.

From Christian antiquity on, some authors have imputed to Origen the doctrine of *apokatastasis*, the restoration of all things and, with it, the ultimate conversion of the demons and even of Satan and, consequently, the finitude of hell. This was not the only objection, but it was the most weighty one.

In a lecture that he gave in 1950 in Lyons[7] on the subject of two homilies by Origen on a verse from the prophet Jeremiah (20:7), which is about God's "pedagogical lying" (can God "deceive" for educational purposes?), de Lubac shows that Origen's position is much more clearly differentiated than the sentences on the basis of which he was condemned in the sixth century.

Another misgiving about Origen concerns his extensive use of "allegorical interpretation",[8] which shows that he was more of a Platonist and a disciple of the philosopher Philo than a Christian theologian. *History and Spirit*, which is still today the standard reference work on Origen's interpretation of Scripture, refutes this objection. Preliminary sketches for this study were written in the form of introductions to the editions of *Origen's Homilies on Genesis* (1943) and *Exodus* (1947) that were published in the series *Sources chrétiennes*. Similarly, in 1947 de Lubac published his highly regarded essay "'Typologie' et 'Allégorisme'", which defended the commonly misunderstood concept of *allegory* against all kinds of distorted interpretations and put it in the proper light as the traditional distinguishing feature of the theological interpretation of Scripture. For the 1948 commemorative volume in honor of Cavallera, de Lubac wrote an essay about the medi-

---

[7] Henri de Lubac, "'Tu m'as trompé, Seigneur': Le Commentaire d'Origene dur Jérémie, XX, 7", in *Mémorial Joseph Chaine* (Lyons: Faculté catholique, 1950). Reprinted in *Recherches dans la foi: Trois études sur Origène, Saint Anselme, et la philosophie chrétienne* (Paris: Beauchesne, 1979), pp. 9–78.

[8] See below, pp. 191–93.

eval distich, or couplet, that summarizes the teaching about
the fourfold sense of Scripture in an easily memorized verse.
Together with the studies on Origen, this essay already intro-
duces the leitmotiv for the great four-volume study *Exégèse
médiévale*.[9]

In 1950—just in time, before an order from de Lubac's
superiors made it impossible for him to publish theological
books for quite a while—*Histoire et Esprit* appeared, "a peace-
able book in the midst of the battle". In it, de Lubac portrays
the Alexandrian theologian as a man of the Church whose
principles for interpreting Scripture were correct, despite
many exaggerations in particular cases. Origen is not an
innovator, but rather a witness to the Tradition that ultimately
goes back to the Apostle Paul. Despite many similarities to
the thought of the Jewish philosopher Philo of Alexandria
(who died c. A.D. 45 or 50), and despite all his dependence on
the Alexandrian milieu, the entire Christian mystery of salvation distinguishes Origen from Philo at the decisive points.

In writing *Histoire et Esprit*, the author wanted to encourage the proponents of modern historical-critical exegesis to
enter into a dialogue about the interrelationship between
scholarly exegesis and systematic theology. It did not fail to
elicit a positive response. De Lubac was especially pleased that
a Scripture scholar such as Father Hugues Vincent, O.P., a
student of Father Marie-Joseph Lagrange, O.P.,[10] gratefully
conveyed to the author his enthusiasm about the study immediately after the book was released and then also wrote a book

---

[9] Henri de Lubac, *Exégèse médiévale*, 2 vols. (1959–1964). English: *Medieval
Exegesis*, vol. 1, trans. Mark Sebanc (Grand Rapids, Mich.: Eerdmans, 1998);
vol. 2, trans. Edward M. Macierowski (Grand Rapids, Mich.: Eerdmans,
2000).

[10] Marie-Joseph Lagrange, O.P. (1855–1938), exegete, professor in Sala-
manca and Toulouse, and founder of the École biblique in Jerusalem. His most
important work is *La Méthode historique* (1903).

review for the *Revue biblique*. De Lubac published two letters from Father Vincent in the appendix to the anthology *L'Écriture dans la Tradition*.[11] It is perhaps typical of de Lubac's view of historical-critical exegesis that during Father Lagrange's lifetime he had repeatedly suggested that the Dominican priest be named a cardinal in recognition of his accomplishments in theology. Such recognition, in de Lubac's opinion, would have had great symbolic significance. It would not only have confirmed the justification for the existence of scholarly exegetes, but would also have given them an incentive in their work (*ASC*, p. 312), and thus it could have helped to soothe many injured feelings and to relieve much of the tension in the relationship between the Magisterium and the exegetes.

In the midst of the first reactions to the publication of *Histoire et Esprit* came startling news.

Lightning Strikes Fourvière

In early 1950, de Lubac received a letter from the General Superior of the Order, announcing the impending withdrawal of his authorization to teach. The pressure had been increasing during 1948 and 1949. Complaints about de Lubac had arrived from many parts of the world. To make matters worse, his essay entitled "Le mystère du surnaturel" [The mystery of the supernatural], published in *Recherches de Sciences Religieuses*[12] in 1949, added to the turmoil, and instead of bringing about the hoped-for clarification, it only

---

[11] Henri de Lubac, *L'Écriture dans la Tradition* (1966); trans. Luke O'Neill, *Scripture in the Tradition* (New York: Crossroad Publishing, 2000).

[12] *Recherches des Sciences Religieuses* is a scholarly journal published by the Jesuits. De Lubac had been serving as its editor since 1946 but had to give up this office, too, in 1950.

led to even more bitter hostility. The reassurance given by one of the assistants to the General, that they were in a position to defend him against the attacks, would prove to be misleading. Plainly, Father Janssens had been convinced after all by his counselors that the accusations leveled against de Lubac were valid. For now the matter was to remain a secret. But in June of 1950, the thunderbolt struck Fourvière. Five Jesuit Fathers in all were deprived of their authorization to teach. They had to leave Lyons; along with Henri de Lubac, Émile Delaye, Henri Bouillard, Alexandre Durand and Pierre Ganne were banished, to mention only those in Fourvière who were affected. It was debated whether to send de Lubac to Toulouse. Finally he was transferred to Paris, where for a time he led a regular hermit's life in an old building in the backyard of the Jesuit college on the Rue de Sèvres. On the same day that he arrived in Paris, the Encyclical *Humani generis*, which the Pope had promulgated on August 12, appeared in the newspaper *La Croix*. One might surmise that the justification for these disciplinary measures was to some extent provided in this papal encyclical letter. In a room that was still empty, in front of an open trunk, de Lubac read the document and could find out now for himself whether he appeared in it and in what light, and which of his teachings were condemned by it. But behold, despite the one-sidedness and the basic apologetic approach that de Lubac noted in the text, not one single sentence could be understood as being formulated against him directly. In the passage where the encyclical dealt with the question of the supernatural, de Lubac discovered that a well-meaning editor who was familiar with his writings evidently had even re-placed one formula, which might have been construed as critical of him, with words that could have been written by de Lubac himself. The passage that may have been aimed at de Lubac reads: "Others [i.e., other theologians] destroy the genuine 'gratuitousness' of the supernatural order by maintaining that God cannot create any beings endowed with reason without ordering and furthermore calling them to the beatific vision" (DH no. 3891). As a matter of fact, de Lubac was never concerned with any sort of speculations as to whom or what God can create. This thesis was, purely and simply, that the entire Christian Tradition until Saint Thomas Aquinas and, after him, up to the sixteenth century understood (1) that God had created man concretely in such a way that, in his intellectual self-transcendence, he can ultimately attain his happiness only in God himself, and (2) that Thomas Aquinas, of all people, knew nothing about a twofold final destiny of man, namely, one natural and one supernatural.

In fact, the encyclical was not explicit enough for de Lubac's opponents. It contains no defense of the theory of "pure nature". That made no difference, however, and shortly after the encyclical's appearance a further measure was taken against de Lubac, above and beyond the prohibition against teaching and publishing. It was decreed that three of his books, *Surnaturel, Corpus mysticum* and *De la Connaissance de Dieu*—among other publications—were to be removed from the libraries of the Jesuit houses and recalled from the bookstores; furthermore, the issue of the journal *Recherches des Sciences Religieuses* containing his essay "Le Mystère du surnaturel" was to be taken off the shelves in the Jesuit libraries (*ASC*, p. 74).

De Lubac resigned himself to the disciplinary measure that was imposed upon him. From his friends he did not conceal how much it pained him. It could not shake his relationship with Christ, his love for the Church and his gratitude to the Jesuit Order. In a letter to Father Charmot, S.J., dated September 9, 1950, he wrote:

Although the shocks that assaulted me from without also troubled my soul to its depths, they are still powerless against the great and essential things that make up every moment of our lives. The Church is always there, in a motherly way, with her Sacraments and her prayer, with the Gospel that she hands down to us intact, with her Saints who surround us; in short, with Jesus Christ, present among us, whom she gives us even more fully at the moments when she allows us to suffer. No doubt the same promises do not apply to the Society of Jesus, but it is true nevertheless that the Church permeates me with her influence to a great extent precisely through it, and if I had only proved to be more docile, the sources of sanctity would have been opened up to me through it [the Jesuit Order], as they are to any other [Jesuit]. What does all the rest matter in comparison with such benefactions? [13]

Solidarity

De Lubac received encouragement and consolation through numerous expressions of sympathy and solidarity. Hans von Balthasar, who not long before that had struggled to reach his decision to leave the Jesuit Order so as to devote himself to the work of founding the Community of St. John, wrote,

Dear Friend, I could scarcely believe what you have written to me. It is upsetting, completely incomprehensible. Yet this is probably the form of martyrdom that must seal your work. You are already the victor; nothing will stop the continued influence of your ideas. . . . Do not lose courage, keep on working as though nothing had happened. So many friends surround you and want to help you. I will do what I can to make your writings known in German-speaking countries. If

[13] Published in *Bulletin de Littérature Ecclésiastique* 94 (1993): 54f.

you have time, write more [to me in another letter]: Who
has to leave Fourvière? Rondet? Bouillard? I fear that Karl
Rahner is very discouraged now—he, who is almost our only
hope. We must support him; you and he must help one
another. Someone [Martha Gisi] is translating your concluding chapter [from the book *Histoire et Esprit* into German]. It
will appear soon in the series *Christ heute*, with permission
from Aubier. I am praying for you. Be cheerful. Yours as
ever, Balthasar.[14]

Three Books on Buddhism

Whereas the General Superior had followed the innuendoes
of his counselors, the new Provincial Superior of Lyons,
Father André Ravier, took Henri de Lubac's side. He thought
it important that de Lubac should continue to do scholarly
work and to publish. "Since theology was closed to me, we
decided that I should write on Buddhism" (*ASC*, p. 72). And
so it happened. As early as the 1930s, he had collected a
wealth of material and had given lectures on Buddhism in
Lyons. In rapid succession, three volumes on the subject
appeared.[15] [Only one has been translated into English, as
Aspects of Buddhism.] Nevertheless, they are worth reading,
because they offer helpful insights into the discernment of
spirits. This is necessary at a time when well-meaning recognition and in-depth study of another religious tradition is
often accompanied by religious pluralism, which ultimately
equates all religions and thus deprives not only Christianity
but also the other religions of their distinctive qualities. De

---

[14] Quoted from Thomas Krenski, *Hans Urs von Balthasar: Das Gottesdrama*
(1995), pp. 91f.

[15] Henri de Lubac, *Aspects du Bouddhisme*, vol. 1 (1951), trans. George
Lamb, *Aspects of Buddhism* (New York: Sheed & Ward, 1954); *La Rencontre du
bouddhisme et de l'occident* (1952); *Aspects du Bouddhisme: Amida*, vol. 2 (1955).

Lubac admits that dealing with the history of religion gave him a keener sense of the incomparably "new thing" [see Jer 31:22] that came into the world with Christ (*ASC*, p. 32).

The theological faculty, too, headed by the university chancellor, the Archbishop of Lyons, Cardinal Gerlier, helped de Lubac to keep a stiff upper lip after the announcement that his authorization to teach was withdrawn. Understandably, they could not tolerate the interference of the Jesuit Order into the affairs of the faculty without further ado. De Lubac had difficulty convincing his colleagues of the hopelessness of any appeal or protest against the decision of his religious superiors. As he said farewell to Cardinal Gerlier, the prelate told him, "I do not want, of course, to urge you to disobey your superiors; but, you well know, your [professorial] chair is yours; you could resume it each and every time you come back through Lyons" (*ASC*, p. 68). In 1951 Cardinal Gerlier ostentatiously appointed de Lubac his theological advisor.

When de Lubac looked back on the affair after the passage of time, he regretted most the impersonal way in which he had been treated. During those years he was not questioned and had no conversation about the essential issue with anyone stationed in Rome, whether an ecclesiastical authority or one in the Society of Jesus. No one told him what he had been accused of, nor did anybody ever request the equivalent of a "*retractatio*", an explanation or the recantation of a particular statement. In the spring of 1953, when he finally saw the Father General, he avoided any discussion of the fundamental question or of the individual facts of the case (see *ASC*, p. 75).

Steps toward Reconciliation

In 1953, de Lubac returned to Lyons. He lived in the Jesuit house in the Rue Sala. Toward the end of that same year, through the mediation of Cardinal Gerlier, de Lubac was allowed to begin teaching again, although not on a regular basis as a member of the theology faculty; at least he could give a few lectures on a nontheological subject.

In the same year, he succeeded again in getting an expressly theological book approved by the censor: *Méditation sur l'Église*.[16] It was not written for specialists and is therefore suitable for a wider readership. It developed out of talks that de Lubac gave at conferences for priests in the years 1946 through 1949. Therefore, it was not prompted by the affair in 1950 or written in self-defense; rather, its release had been delayed by what had happened after 1950.

It contains, among others, the chapter entitled "The Man of the Church", a brilliant description of what it truly means to belong to the Church. Herbert Vorgrimler[17] is right in saying that these pages can be read as a program for the theological work of Henri de Lubac. They formulate that ideal of living in and with the Church to which he was committed for his entire life. This portrait begins, characteristically, with a citation from Origen:

> "For myself," said Origen, "I desire to be truly ecclesiastic".
> He thought—and rightly—that there was no other way of being a Christian in the full sense. And anyone who is possessed by a similar desire will not find it enough to be

---

[16] Henri de Lubac, *Méditation sur l'Église* (1953). In 1968, Hans Urs von Balthasar produced a second German translation of this book, entitled *Die Kirche: Eine Betrachtung*. In 1956, Sheed & Ward published an English translation, from the second French edition, by Michael Mason. It has been reprinted as *The Splendor of the Church* (San Francisco: Ignatius Press, 1986, 1999); cited as *SpCh*.

[17] Herbert Vorgrimler, "Henri de Lubac", in Herbert Vorgrimler and Robert Vander Gucht, eds., *Bilanz der Theologie im 20. Jahrhundert: Bahnbrechende Theologen* [Balance-sheet of twentieth-century theology: groundbreaking theologians] (1970), p. 200.

loyal and obedient, to perform exactly everything demanded by his profession of the Catholic faith. Such a man will have fallen in love with the beauty of the House of God; the Church will have stolen his heart. She is his spiritual native country, his "mother and his brethren", and nothing that concerns her will leave him indifferent or detached; he will root himself in her soil, form himself in her likeness, and make himself one with her experience. He will feel himself rich with her wealth; he will be aware that through her and her alone he participates in the unshakeableness of God. It will be from her that he learns how to live and die. Far from passing judgment on her, he will allow her to judge him, and he will agree gladly to all the sacrifices demanded by her unity (*SpCh*, pp. 241–42).

The years 1955 and 1956 brought further relaxation of the disciplinary measures. Again at the request of Cardinal Gerlier, a concession was made in 1956 for de Lubac to give lectures from then on *ad experimentum* at the Catholic University on the subjects of Hinduism and Buddhism.

Man and the Idea of God

In 1956, the third, expanded edition of *De la Connaissance de Dieu* was published under the title *Sur les Chemins de Dieu*.[18] It presents the thesis that man has a living, natural, pre-conceptual awareness of God's presence; de Lubac speaks of the "idea of God in man", which of course should not be understood as though God were present in man. It is precisely the absence of what man necessarily desires as the fulfillment of his longing that causes him to become aware of this idea of God, rather than a sense of being called by God. Critics

---

[18] On this subject, see in particular pp. 139–58, below.

[of earlier editions] had charged that the "natural theology" that de Lubac suggests aphoristically in this book, without developing it systematically, was not distinguished clearly enough from positions that the Magisterium had condemned as ontologism, agnosticism or fideism.[19] Without essentially modifying his view, de Lubac had defended his arguments against these attacks by numerous additions and clarifications and especially by citing a wealth of documentation from the history of theology. Martin Lenk has minutely examined de Lubac's revisions. His conclusion: de Lubac's paradoxical mode of thinking, which he learned from the Church Fathers and which also comes to light in his reflections on the idea of God in man, collided with the system of natural theology that was part and parcel of the Neo-Scholastic theology taught in the seminaries, because de Lubac did not fit into that framework.

Exégèse médiévale

In April 1956, de Lubac began composing the first volume of *Exégèse médiévale*. He had been gathering material for it in the form of countless slips of paper containing excerpts. De Lubac had systematically plowed through the *Patrologia Latina* and *Graeca*[20] and had copied out the pertinent passages. Yet the sometimes unreliable volumes from the Migne collection

[19] Fideism (Latin *fides*, "faith") is a theological outlook that considers all religious truth to be accessible only in the trusting act of faith and rejects arguments from reason. This perspective, as well as its opposite, rationalism (Latin *ratio*, "reason"), was condemned by the First Vatican Council (1869–1870).

[20] *Patrologia Latina* (PL) and *Patrologia Graeca* (PG) were published by Jacques-Paul Migne (1800–1875). This collection of patristic writings (217 volumes by the Latin Church Fathers and 162 volumes by the Greek Fathers) only reproduces earlier editions and therefore is considered "uncritical".

were not the only basis for his work. Whenever possible, he used the critical editions and, with astonishing erudition, often tracked down quite obscure editions of little-known authors and gleaned their observations and statements on the question of the Christian understanding of Scripture. De Lubac himself gives us an insight into the plan and the realization of this monumental, four-volume work, which finally appeared during the years 1959–1964.

> It was at Corenc, near Grenoble, [while I was staying] with the Sisters of Providence, that I set to work in the early days of April 1956. At first [envisioned] in modest dimensions, the book swelled beyond measure. I warmed up to the game and amused myself with classifying into little parcels the bits and pieces of texts (somewhat like what I had done for *Corpus mysticum*); I made some curious discoveries, glimpsed unexpected ramifications, became attached to some little known or poorly known figures. Along the way I became more and more strongly aware of *the essential nature of the extraordinary connection*, always threatened but always maintained or reestablished within the [Universal] Church, *between the two Testaments*; I saw it more and more clearly dominating the whole history and the whole doctrine of the Church, from the first century to our own time. . . . I admired the marvelous synthesis of the whole Christian faith, thought and spirituality contained in the so-called doctrine of the "four senses [of Scripture]", grasped as it welled forth. I was happy working to do justice in that way [i.e., through my research] to one of the central elements of the Catholic tradition, so grossly unappreciated in modern times and nevertheless still the bearer of promises for renewal (*ASC*, pp. 83–84).

In March 1958, thanks to the persistent efforts of Father Agostino Bea, S.J., the Pope's confessor, and of the Jesuit Provincial, they managed to bypass the Roman officials and present to the Pope four books by de Lubac, together with a devoted dedicatory letter by the author. Pius XII promptly sent cordial words of thanks and encouraged de Lubac. The Jesuit General, Father Janssens, unsure of what to do, was unwilling to look at the letter because it was not official. Janssens, incorrectly informed about de Lubac's real specialty, thought that with permission to give lectures on Hinduism and Buddhism the original *status quo ante* had been restored. De Lubac had to set him right and point out that he had also taught fundamental theology on the Faculty of Theology. Finally, a conciliatory letter from the General arrived, which spoke of misunderstandings and of the fact that God turns all things to the good for those who love him (*ASC*, pp. 90–91).

In December 1958, Cardinal Gerlier brought back from Rome verbal approval for de Lubac to resume lecturing. The Father General now said that he had never removed de Lubac from his professorial chair. In reply to an unofficial inquiry, the Congregation for Seminaries expressed amazement that authorization to teach should be requested for someone who had had it since 1929, without its ever having been withdrawn.

In a letter dated June 19, 1959, the General asked de Lubac to take up again his teaching duties in the Faculty of Theology. From November 1959 to March 1, 1960, de Lubac was responsible once more for a few lectures, but he then asked to be relieved of these duties. A few months later he received from the Faculty the title of honorary professor [*honoris causa*].

At around the same time as his rehabilitation, a great honor was awarded to de Lubac on the secular plane. On December 5, 1958, he was elected a member of the *Académie des sciences morales et politiques*, one of the five branches of the *Institut de France*.

Dispute with Hans Küng

It is interesting that Henri de Lubac considered himself obliged in 1958 to defend his confrere Henri Bouillard against Hans Küng.[21] The latter had first accepted help from Bouillard while writing his 1957 doctoral thesis on Karl Barth,[22] but one year later he severely and a bit condescendingly criticized his mentor's interpretation of Barth. In his study of Barth,[23] which took a very favorable view of the Protestant theologian, Küng had tried to prove, from just a few passages, that Barth was advocating a position, in regard to the doctrine of justification, that is acceptable to Catholics. Bouillard's perspective[24] was more differentiated and skeptical, and of course Küng accused it of hampering the ecumenical movement.

Bouillard's finding was this: despite isolated remarks about the "creative character" of grace, in Barth's view the process of justification ultimately remains something extrinsic to man. It is merely testimony to the justification that objectively has already occurred in Christ, but it in no way makes man a new being.

Henri de Lubac pointed out that it does not serve the cause of ecumenism when supposed points of agreement are prematurely claimed, without working out the real meaning

[21] Henri de Lubac, "Zum katholischen Dialog mit Karl Barth", *Dokumente* 14 (1958): 448–54.

[22] Karl Barth (1886–1968), Protestant theologian, was a proponent of "dialectical theology". His principal work is the multi-volume *Kirchliche Dogmatik* [Church dogmatics] (1932–1967).

[23] Hans Küng, *Rechtfertigung: Die Lehre Karl Barths und eine katholische Besinnung* [Justification: The teaching of Karl Barth, and a Catholic commentary] (1957).

[24] Henri Bouillard, *Karl Barth*, vol. 1, *Genèse et Évolution de la Théologie dialectique*, vols. 2 and 3, *Parole de Dieu et existence humaine* (1958). See the review by Küng himself in *Dokumente* 14 (1958): 236f.

of Saint Paul's statements with sufficient care, and without taking seriously enough the Decree on Justification of the Council of Trent.

Collaborating on the
Second Vatican Council

On January 25, 1959, the last day of the World Octave of Prayer for the Reunion of Christians, the newly elected Pope John XXIII surprised the cardinals present in the Basilica of Saint Paul Outside the Walls with the announcement that he intended to convoke a council.

On May 17 (Pentecost Sunday) of the same year, the preparatory commission was established, under the direction of Cardinal Tardini. One year later, the second phase of the preparations began: ten commissions and two secretariats were set up. Most of the commissions (working committees) corresponded to the areas of competence of the various Roman Congregations. It was the task of the preparatory commissions to collate the suggestions of the bishops and theologians and the recommendations from the commissions and then to compose drafts (*schemata*) for the documents that the Council would then debate and finally approve. The members of these commissions, bishops and theological advisors (*consultores*), were selected by the heads of the commissions (who were the prefects of the respective congregations), or they were appointed by the Pope personally. As a member of one of the preparatory commissions, de Lubac also became a *peritus* (literally: someone with experience, "expert") for the Council.

Two Questionable *Periti* and a Distrustful Cardinal

In August 1960, de Lubac read by chance in the newspaper
(*ASC*, p. 116) that he, along with the Dominican priest Yves
Congar, had been appointed by the Pope to the Theological
Commission, which was headed by the Prefect of the Holy
Office, Cardinal Ottaviani. At the time of the Fourvière
affair, Giuseppe Roncalli (later Pope John XXIII) has been
papal nuncio in Paris, and he had followed the matter very
attentively. He certainly had not been consulted and had by
no means agreed to the dismissal of de Lubac and Congar
from their teaching positions. The first positive signal from
the nuncio-turned-Pope was a considerable donation to the
series *Sources chrétiennes*, which, being a production of Fourvière, had also come under suspicion. Now the appointment
of the two theologians from the Jesuit and Dominican Orders
to a preparatory commission for the Council could be interpreted as a sign that the Pope wanted to put an end to the
affair and that he viewed the two theologians—representatives of all those who had suffered injustice—as being completely rehabilitated.

In his memoir, *At the Service of the Church*, de Lubac
chivalrously spreads a mantle of silence over the particulars of
the work in that commission.[1] From the few recollections
that he has published, we can infer that he not only had great
difficulty with the working methods of a commission and
with the sort of documents that it was supposed to draft, but
also that Cardinal Ottaviani plainly was nowhere near as
convinced as the Pope of de Lubac's reliability, and consequently hindered his work. In 1961, he was asked as a mem-

[1] See Lenk, p. 106 (Martin Lenk had access to unpublished material, as
well). See also Klaus Wittstadt, ed., *Geschichte des Zweiten Vatikanischen Konzils
(1959–1965)*, vol. 1 (1997), pp. 273–78.

ber of the theological commission for an opinion on the "various kinds of knowledge of God". Since this opinion was never discussed and served no other purpose, de Lubac could not help suspecting that it had been devised as a test of his orthodoxy (*ASC*, p. 117).

Nevertheless, he succeeded in staving off a condemnation of Teilhard de Chardin, which was demanded by one group, as well as in clarifying his own theological position, which had been falsely reported. In order to accomplish this, however, de Lubac had to throw onto the scales the entire weight of the theological authority that he had recently regained: he threatened to resign from the commission and to state his reasons for doing so, should it happen that his objections were not taken into account.

Direct and Indirect Influence

De Lubac's collaboration in one of the subcommissions was crowned with greater success: it was the group that drew up Schema 13, which served as the foundation for the Pastoral Constitution *Gaudium et spes*. As the author of *The Drama of Atheist Humanism*, he was an expert on questions of atheism. He became an influential advisor both for Archbishop Wojtyla and for Cardinal König, who headed the Secretariat for Non-believers. Articles 19 through 22 of *Gaudium et spes*, which deal with modern atheism and the proper response of the Church, clearly show that they were inspired by de Lubac, down to the formulation of individual sentences.

De Lubac had some direct influence on the composition of the conciliar documents. He had an even greater indirect influence, however, in that he had made such a name for himself as a theologian that many bishops had read his books; through their mediation much of the letter and the spirit of de Lubac's work also became the letter and the spirit of the Council. According to Karl Heinz Neufeld,

> what is decisive for an ecclesiastical assembly is not so much the discussions and the protocols of the deliberations; the lasting accomplishments are the official declarations that have been approved. Since de Lubac is directly cited in them here and there as a source, it is evident that the Council made some of his ideas its own, even though he is not in every case the only one who developed or championed a particular conviction. Nonetheless the theologian had his turn in making suggestions which acquainted the Council Fathers with new perspectives or else vigorously promoted them. In most cases he had discovered in the Church Fathers or in later theology decisive reasons and had proven that certain ideas had already had right of domicile in the early Church."[2]

Pope Paul VI was not only acquainted with de Lubac's books on Scripture as a witness to divine revelation and on the essential characteristics of the Christian interpretation of Scripture but also valued them and considered them important for the recently completed Dogmatic Constitution on Divine Revelation, *Dei Verbum*. We can tell this from two symbolic gestures that Karl Heinz Neufeld recalls. On November 18, 1965, the Pope invited de Lubac, along with several other theologians, to concelebrate Mass with him on the occasion of the approval of the Constitution on Divine Revelation. Secondly, after the ecumenical celebration with the non-Catholic observers at the conclusion of the Council, he invited Henri de Lubac, together with Oscar Cullmann[3]

---

[2] Karl Heinz Neufeld, "Henri de Lubac S.J. als Konzilstheologe: Zur Vollendung seines 90. Lebensjahres", *Theologisch-praktische Quartalschrift* 134 (1986): 153.

[3] Oscar Cullmann (1902–1999), a Lutheran exegete and theologian who taught for many years at a Calvinist divinity school in Basel, Switzerland, was an official observer at the Council.

and Jean Guitton,[4] to dine with him in the papal apartments on the following Sunday.

Commentaries on the Conciliar documents

Three years later, de Lubac published a detailed commentary on the Preamble and chapter 1 of the Dogmatic Constitution on Divine Revelation.[5] In it he emphasizes the personal character of God's revelation in Jesus Christ. *Dei Verbum*, the Word of God, the words that open the Constitution on Divine Revelation and also state its theme, do not refer in the first place to Sacred Scripture, but rather to the Person of the One-who-reveals, to Jesus Christ, the very Word of God, in whom God has spoken to us in the fullness of time. Jesus Christ is the one source of revelation; Scripture and Tradition are not in themselves sources of revelation, but rather modes in which it is communicated.

De Lubac commented on the conciliar statements about the Church in various essays and articles that he collected in 1967 under the title *Paradoxe et Mystère de l'Église*.[6] The idea for this anthology came from Hans Urs von Balthasar, who with a translation of some of these essays on the Church as *Geheimnis aus dem wir leben* (1968), began publishing de Lubac's works in German.

De Lubac was asked to write an introduction to the Pastoral Constitution *Gaudium et spes* as well. A series of lectures on the subject eventually became the little volume entitled *Athéisme et sens de l'homme: Une double requête de Gaudium et*

[4] Jean Guitton (1901–1999), Catholic author and philosopher, taught at the Sorbonne in Paris from 1955 on.

[5] Henri de Lubac, *Le Révélation divine* (1968).

[6] English edition: Henri de Lubac, *The Church: Paradox and Mystery*, trans. James R. Dunne (New York: Alba House, 1969); here cited as *CPM*.

spes (Atheism and the meaning of man: a twofold application of *GS*; 1968).

Member of the Secretariat for Non-believers and of the International Theological Commission

While the Council was still in session, de Lubac was appointed to the Secretariat for Non-Christians and the Secretariat for Non-believers, which the Pope established in 1964 and 1965, respectively. Membership in these panels did not mean much extra work for him, but his impressions of the prevailing tone in the Commission for Non-believers made it quite clear to him how far postconciliar theology was beginning to drift from what he considered to be Catholic theology. He could not condone the uncritical adoption of a purely sociological way of viewing the Church and the internal trends toward secularization. He noted, however, that he and his opinions were soon marginalized.

In 1969, Henri de Lubac was also recruited for the newly constituted International Theological Commission.[7] Other members of this circle included Hans Urs von Balthasar, Karl Rahner, Joseph Ratzinger, Rudolf Schnackenburg and Heinz Schürmann. A presentation for the Theological Commission on the topic of nature and grace formed the basis for the book *Petite catéchèse sur Nature et Grâce*,[8] in which de Lubac's principal statements about the doctrine of grace are once again collected, along with some clarifications.

[7] The International Theological Commission, an advisory panel to the pope, is an adjunct to the Congregation for the Doctrine of the Faith, which is headed by its prefect. The Commission is made up of theologians of different schools and nationalities and is appointed for a five-year term.

[8] Henri de Lubac, *Petite catéchèse sur nature et grâce* (Paris, 1980); trans. Richard Arnandez, *A Brief Catechesis on Nature and Grace* (San Francisco: Ignatius Press, 1984).

Defense of Teilhard de Chardin

One of the great challenges for theology are the findings of the modern natural sciences, especially the question whether evolutionary theory can be reconciled with belief in creation, the Incarnation of God and salvation in Christ. The name Pierre Teilhard de Chardin[9] is connected with the bold attempt to take up the scientific view of man from the perspective of theology and to combine the two disciplines in a comprehensive interpretation that interrelates natural history and salvation history and concentrates all of reality upon the central figure of Christ.

Teilhard de Chardin, who was both a theologian and an experienced natural scientist, made the idea of *development* the central concept of theology itself by outlining an "evolutionary Christology". The whole cosmos is constructed with a view to bringing forth man. The development of mankind, in turn, advances toward the Incarnation of God, which takes place at a certain stage of development and becomes the point of departure for a new dynamic. God in Christ is the center of the whole cosmos, which advances toward its "Omega point", its definitive goal in the cosmic Christ.

Teilhard's theories were disputed from the very beginning. In particular, his interpretation of original sin (in the sense of a "counter-evolution") is theologically unacceptable. His stays in east Asia were not only for the purpose of research, but also served as a kind of exile. At the command of his

[9] Pierre Teilhard de Chardin, S.J. (1881–1955), entered the Jesuit Order in 1899. He served from 1905 to 1908 as a physics teacher in a Jesuit college in Cairo. In 1922, he was appointed professor of geology in Paris, and for more than twenty years he traveled in the Far East doing research. In 1929, he took part in the discovery of Peking Man, the oldest example of a human ancestor known at that time. He returned to Paris in 1948 and died on Easter Sunday, 1955, in New York.

Order, not one of his philosophical or theological works was allowed to appear in print during his lifetime, and as late as the spring of 1961, de Lubac was reminded that it was not permitted to write anything about Teilhard. This was to change soon.

In the months leading up to the Council, a broad consensus had formed that wanted to see Teilhard de Chardin's writings condemned. In early summer of 1961, de Lubac was quite unexpectedly assigned by the governing council of the Order itself to compose a book in defense of Teilhard as quickly as possible. The book appeared soon after,[10] in early 1962. Henri de Lubac did not set out to present those aspects of Teilhard's thought that involve the natural sciences, but rather focused on his mysticism, which is central to all of his thinking. De Lubac presents evidence for the ecclesial character and the basic missionary impulse of his friend and confrere, without, of course, ignoring the limitations in his work. Teilhard wanted to bring Christ closer to the men of the age of science and to overcome the lack of a common language between natural science and theology, as well as to bridge the chasm between faith and knowledge. In doing so, he set foot on new territory, and that always involves risks. His endeavor, according to de Lubac, deserved not only a more accurate judgment but also recognition and thanks.

Although it had been requested and approved by the superiors of the Jesuit Order, the book almost ended up on the list of forbidden books. For de Lubac, it resulted at any rate in a *monitum* (warning) from the Magisterium, *L'Osservatore Romano* published an anonymous critique, and for a while the book could not be reprinted or translated! Now, however, for

[10] Henri de Lubac, *La Pensée religieuse du Père Teilhard de Chardin* (1962); trans. René Hague, *The Religion of Teilhard de Chardin* (New York: Desclée Company, 1967).

the first time, the Jesuit General, Father Janssens, decisively took de Lubac's side. In a letter dated August 27, 1962, he wrote in conclusion: "It was my judgment that your book served the Church and the truth, and I wanted it to be published. I have not regretted this decision" (cited in *ASC*, p. 106). The General's fundamental attitude toward de Lubac had changed altogether as of the year 1961. It seemed that a great burden had fallen from his shoulders, and from then on he showed every possible sign of good will in dealing with de Lubac. The prohibition against publishing a new edition of the first apologia prompted de Lubac to write another book immediately.[11] After two more years came a third.[12] Finally, this was followed by the publication of a poem by Teilhard that he had written during the First World War, together with a long commentary by de Lubac, which elaborates and evaluates Teilhard's Mariology, which is contained therein.[13] Not the least important in bringing about a just appreciation of the great Jesuit and naturalist was the publication of an annotated edition of his correspondence with Maurice Blondel (1965)[14] and of his personal correspondence from Cairo,[15] which brings him to life and acquaints the reader with him as a young naturalist with deep faith who is certain that he will

[11] Henri de Lubac, *La Prière du Père Teilhard de Chardin* (1964; 2nd ed. 1967); trans. René Hague, *Teilhard de Chardin: The Man and His Meaning* (New York: Hawthorn Books, 1965).

[12] Henri de Lubac, *Teilhard, missionnaire et apologiste* (1966); trans. Anthony Buono, *Teilhard Explained* (New York: Paulist Press, 1968).

[13] Pierre Teilhard de Chardin, *L'Éternel Féminin* (1968); trans. René Hague, *The Eternal Feminine: A Study on the Poem by Teilhard de Chardin, Followed by Teilhard and the Problems of Today* (New York: Harper & Row, 1971).

[14] English edition: Pierre Teilhard de Chardin and Maurice Blondel, *Correspondence*, with notes and commentary by Henri de Lubac, trans. William Whitman (New York: Herder and Herder, 1967).

[15] Pierre Teilhard de Chardin, *Lettres d'Egypte* (1963); English edition: *Letters from Egypt, 1905–1908*, preface by Henri de Lubac, trans. Mary Ilford (New York: Herder and Herder, 1965).

"find God in all things". A few months before the end of the Council, de Lubac had been asked by Father Boyer (his and Teilhard's most vehement opponent) to speak about Teilhard "sympathetically" (!) on September 10, 1965, in the great hall of the *Palazzo della Cancelleria* at the solemn concluding session of the Thomistic congress headed by Boyer. The invitation was extended at the express wish of Pope Paul VI (*ASC*, p. 108). This could well be regarded as a particular expression of appreciation for Teilhard and as the endpoint of a downright fanatical anti-Teilhard campaign.

Another event during the conciliar period was de Lubac's fiftieth jubilee as a religious, in October 1963. On that occasion, students and friends dedicated to him a three-volume *Festschrift* with the significant title *L'Homme devant Dieu* (Man in the presence of God), which appeared as volumes 56–58 in the series *Théologie*. In it, de Lubac's work is comprehensively evaluated or else taken as the point of departure for further special studies. The first volume contains essays on the subject of "Exegesis and Patristics", the second volume is subtitled "From the Middle Ages to the Enlightenment Period", and finally the third volume opens up "Present-day Perspectives".

A Book That Came Too Soon

During the intervals between the sessions of the Council, in the time not taken up by his defense of Teilhard, de Lubac set to work on finishing the fourth volume of *Exégèse médiévale*, which appeared in 1964. (He had already submitted the first two volumes in 1959 and the third volume in 1961.) There is no other way of putting it: this work, with its wealth of material, came much too soon. The theological discussion of the day was overly concerned with the approval of historical-critical exegesis, which had been obtained at last, for it to be able to arouse much interest in a work that places this exegesis, without devaluing it in the least, within the larger overall theological context. Only three decades later, apparently, would there be a new and broader-based understanding for what de Lubac had already presented masterfully back then.

De Lubac nicknamed his two books[16] from the year 1965 his "twins"; they take up again the theme of *Surnaturel*, respond to its critiques and clarify many things, without any essential changes in content from the 1946 and 1949 versions. "One, *Le Mystère du surnaturel*, develops point by point, in the same order and without changing the least point of doctrine, the article published under that title in *Recherches* in 1949. . . . The second, *Augustinisme et théologie moderne*, reproduced with similar fidelity the first part of the old *Surnaturel* [1946], enlarging it with new [citations]" (*ASC*, p. 123). The philosopher and expert Thomist Étienne Gilson (1884-1978) wrote on June 21, 1965, to de Lubac: "*Le Mystère du surnaturel*, which I have just thoroughly enjoyed reading from cover to cover, is absolutely perfect. . . . You've said all that can be said, particularly the very important counsel that eventually there comes a time when one must be silent. It truly is a mystery that is at issue here."[17]

The Church in Crisis?

A short four years after the conclusion of the Council, de Lubac publicly complained about the one-sided reception of

[16] They were published together in German with the title *Die Freiheit der Gnade*, vols. 1 and 2. English edition: *Augustinianism and Modern Theology*, trans. Lancelot Sheppard (New York: Herder and Herder, 1969), and *The Mystery of the Supernatural*, trans. Rosemary Sheed (New York: Herder and Herder, 1967).

[17] *Letters of Étienne Gilson to Henri de Lubac*, annotated by Father de Lubac, trans. Mary Emily Hamilton (San Francisco: Ignatius Press, 1988), p. 91.

the documents of the assembly of the Universal Church that had just taken place.

At the University of Saint Louis (Missouri), de Lubac gave a lecture that was published in expanded form under the title *L'Église dans la crise actuelle* (The Church in the present crisis),[18] 1969. De Lubac observed a break with Tradition, as if theology had come into its own only with the Second Vatican Council. In *Entretien autour de Vatican II*, he talks about an "underground council" [*para-concile*] that was active as early as 1962 and went public in 1968, resolutely determined to distance itself from the preceding Councils of Trent and Vatican I.[19] The Pastoral Constitution *Gaudium et spes* had recommended an "openness to the world", which did not mean conformity to the world. Rather, it was necessary to overcome an anxious attitude whereby the Church selfishly withdraws "into a sort of quarantine" and leaves mankind to its own fate. "Yet don't we find now", de Lubac writes, "that, quite to the contrary, on the basis of a massive deception, this 'opening' leads to forgetting about salvation, to alienation from the Gospel, to rejection of Christ's cross, to a way that leads to secularism, to self-indulgence in faith and morals, in short, to dissolution in worldliness, abdication, indeed a loss of identity, which means a betrayal of our duty toward the world?" (*L'Église dans la crise actuelle*; German ed.: *Krise zum Heil?*, p. 29).

---

[18] An English translation of this work does not yet exist, but an abridged version is available: "The Church in Crisis", *Theology Digest* 17 (1969): 312–25.

[19] Henri de Lubac, *Entretien autour de Vatican II: Souvenirs et réflexions* (Paris: Catholique-Cerf, 1985), pp. 33–57; abridged English translation: Henri de Lubac and Angelo Scola, *De Lubac: A Theologian Speaks* (Los Angeles: Twin Circles Publishing, 1985), pp. 14–15. The abridgement is here cited as *ATS*.

Twilight Years in Paris

In 1974, the Jesuits closed the *lycée* and the college in Lyons-Fourvière, and de Lubac again moved to Paris, where he spent his twilight years. Despite his advancing age, Henri de Lubac had the gift of an astonishing creativity. He was able to finish a series of book projects. Not until October 1986 did he suffer a stroke, which, although it left its mark on him physically, did not detract from his presence of mind. A second stroke in Advent of 1989 completely deprived him of his ability to speak.

For de Lubac, the 1970s were also overshadowed by many disappointments. He had helped in so many ways to prepare for the Second Vatican Council and only a few years before had had to defend himself against the accusation that he was an innovator, yet now he was suddenly considered the proponent of an old, supposedly obsolete theology.

Disappointments

For his eightieth birthday, on February 20, 1976, de Lubac received a handwritten letter[1] from Pope Paul VI. He showed it to the superior of the house, but he did not even want to look at it, and his Provincial would not read it either. De

[1] The text of the letter, in the original Latin and in English translation, is in *ASC*, pp. 379–82.

Lubac was pained by the lack of interest, but even more by the trouble that it caused, since the letter was obviously composed in such a way that the writer in Rome must have assumed that the addressee would allow his superior to read it as well. Then, when the editor of *France catholique* learned about the existence of the letter, without any help from de Lubac, and asked de Lubac to publish it, de Lubac immediately received permission from his superiors to do so. On March 25, 1977, the letter was published. In the monthly newsletter of the Society of Jesus for May of that same year there was only a brief notice of it. Of course, this gave the impression that de Lubac himself had indiscreetly launched its publication.

Another example: In 1978 the (new) editors of *Sources chrétiennes* asked de Lubac to write a theological introduction to the planned edition of *De sacerdotio* (On the priesthood), by John Chrysostom, the first significant presentation of a theology of the priestly ministry. De Lubac composed a text in which he limited himself to discussing the dogmatic aspects of the work by the great Archbishop of Constantinople and only incidentally touched on the spiritual and theological aspects. Thus de Lubac emphasizes the continuity of the development in the theology of the priesthood from its New Testament origins onward. De Lubac rejects the claim that over the course of Church history the understanding of the priesthood had been falsified and that, between the New Testament witness and Chrysostom, what originally had been a minister of the Word had become a cultic minister, that is, a priest in the pagan sense. Nor does he fail to mention that, according to Chrysostom, as throughout the Tradition of the Church, the restriction of the priesthood to the male sex is not a Church precept, but rather is of divine right, founded on the will of Jesus as he instituted the sacrament, inasmuch as the priest represents Christ, the Bridegroom of the Church. When the volume appeared then, in 1978, as number 272 in the series *Sources chrétiennes*, de Lubac's theological introduction was not included in it. A group of influential people had opposed it. De Lubac did not want to jeopardize the release of the volume, and so he withdrew his manuscript and published it as an essay in an academic journal (*ASC*, p. 153).[2]

Whereas de Lubac was regarded by proponents of a self-styled progressive trend as a theologian who had meanwhile become hopelessly obsolete, there was, on the other hand, no lack of critics who claimed that he was primarily responsible for the onset of the crisis in the Church. In 1975 someone mailed de Lubac photocopied excerpts from the book entitled *Gethsemane*, by the Archbishop of Genoa, Cardinal Siri. The cardinal denounced "the historical conscience", "hermeneutics" and "the existential reference" as hallmarks of a theology leading to destruction, for which de Lubac was chiefly to blame, along with Karl Rahner and Jacques Maritain. De Lubac resolutely defended himself against these charges in a letter dated November 15, 1975, "with the expression of my grieved amazement" (*ASC*, pp. 168-69). Without entering into a discussion with Siri, de Lubac referred to the approval of his work by Pope Pius XII and to the favorable judgment of Étienne Gilson. De Lubac's demand that Siri should publicly retract his charges was not met. Instead, *Gethsemane* was translated into French and other languages, as well.[3]

---

[2] Henri de Lubac, "Le Dialogue sur le sacerdoce de Saint Jean Chrysostome", *Nouvelle revue théologique* 100 (1978): 822-31.

[3] Cardinal Joseph Siri, *Gethsemane: Reflections on the Contemporary Theological Movement* (Chicago: Franciscan Herald Press, 1981).

Late Works

From the list of de Lubac's publications in the 1970s, we should single out in particular two works that deal with two entirely different personalities from the history of theology. Neither of them had been correctly appreciated until then: Joachim of Fiore, with respect to the disastrous history of his influence, and Pico della Mirandola[4] with respect to his indisputable ecclesial sense and orthodoxy. *Pic de la Mirandole* was published in 1974 and *La postérité spirituelle de Joachim de Fiore* in 1979–1981. Neither work is available in English translation.

Despite a series of recent monographs about Pico, de Lubac considered him to be as misunderstood as ever. He found that even very conscientious historians of the Renaissance lacked a real understanding of the great Christian humanist, a deficit that he once before had had to point out in connection with Erasmus of Rotterdam. The materials for his Pico monograph, de Lubac writes, were collected over the course of forty years, in which he was especially fond of dealing with this "young and old friend" of his in his free time. De Lubac sees (and reveres) in Pico the representative of a truly Catholic philosopher who takes the Incarnation seriously in its far-reaching consequences and little by little incorporates it into his philosophical thought. It was not only that Pico passionately supported Origen and, contrary to the medieval understanding of Origen's condemnation, defended the thesis that it was more reasonable to believe that Origen was saved than that he had been damned; Pico was one of those who understood the essence of the spiritual interpreta-

---

[4] Pico della Mirandola (1461–1494) was a Renaissance philosopher. [See chap. 3 of Henri de Lubac, *Theology in History: Part One: The Light of Christ* (San Francisco: Ignatius Press, 1996).]

tion of Scripture founded by Paul and the Church Fathers upon the hermeneutic principle that the Old and New Testaments are connected, and also put it into practice. Whereas de Lubac stands up for thinkers like Origen and Pico unreservedly (without overlooking their weaknesses) and makes no secret of his sympathy with them, his relationship to Joachim of Fiore is rather ambivalent.

Previously, in the third volume of *Exégèse médiévale* (1961, pp. 437–558), de Lubac had presented Joachim's teaching in connection with his principles for interpreting Scripture. By the end of the 1970s, he was able to complete a two-volume monograph, using the plentiful material on the history of Joachim's influence that he had collected. At first, de Lubac confesses, the work of this peculiar Calabrian abbot, the forceful originality of his exegesis and also the breadth of his visions fascinated him. And he is even ready to admit "that a kind of semi-Joachimism (perhaps less unfaithful to the aim of Joachim himself) . . . was, on the contrary, the tentative search for what was to be the normal development of Catholic tradition . . . the discovery by the Church herself, all along her pilgrimage, of the perpetual fruitfulness of the Gospel, from which she draws, with each new situation, . . . *nova et vetera*" [new things and old, see Mt 13:52]. Yet ultimately he sees in him and especially in his intellectual heirs—indeed, in stark contrast to Pico (and also in contrast to Origen)—those fundamental spiritualistic misunderstandings of the biblical message that either explain away or minimize the Incarnation of the Divine Word in history. And so de Lubac's final judgment is a severe one, in which he recognizes that the secularizing tendencies within the Church and the ascendancy of social utopias in it (which he so bitterly laments) are ultimately the heritage of Joachim or else of his intellectual heirs (see *ASC*, p. 157).

De Lubac: A Theologian Speaks—
On the Letter and Spirit of the Council

In the 1980s, the interview became fashionable in theology as well. Henri de Lubac, too, who by then was almost ninety years old, allowed himself to be interviewed by the Italian professor Angelo Scola on the occasion of the twentieth anniversary of the conclusion of the Council.[5]

The judgments and recollections offered spontaneously in a free-wheeling style in this conversation overlap in many respects with what de Lubac recorded also in his literary memoir, *At the Service of the Church*.

The interview deals first with the pre-history of the Council. De Lubac recalls the renewal of theology through a return to the sources: Sacred Scripture and the theology of the Church Fathers. He recapitulates the debate over *Surnaturel* and the Encyclical *Humani generis* and declares that the Council in fact overcame the dualism between nature and grace by speaking explicitly about the one final end of man: God.

Ecclesiological topics take up much of the discussion. In de Lubac's opinion, even the Dogmatic Constitution on the Church *Lumen gentium* receives too little attention. Whereas the Council emphasizes that the Church is essentially a mystery, founded upon the work of Christ, and takes this as the point of departure in explaining her sacramental structure (which includes the importance of the bishop's ministry and of episcopal collegiality in union with the Pope), de Lubac has the impression that purely external organizational questions intruded themselves into the limelight due to pressure from a merely sociological way of looking at the Church. In

---

[5] Henri de Lubac, *Entretien autour de Vatican II: Souvenirs et réflexions* (here cited as *EVII*); abridged English translation: Henri de Lubac and Angelo Scola, *De Lubac: A Theologian Speaks* (*ATS*).

this context, he even cautions against an overemphasis on the national bishops' conferences and their bureaucracies.

Last but not least thought-provoking are de Lubac's remarks on exegesis and hermeneutics and his statement that *Dei Verbum*, which "is also a text about Tradition", has been insufficiently studied and assimilated. The synthesis called for in the document between historical research into the Scriptures and the theological-spiritual interpretation of them has yet to be accomplished. This constitution speaks, furthermore, about "the Old and the New Testaments, which explain each other. Yet above all it is a text about the personal character of divine revelation in Jesus Christ" (*EVII*, p. 87; see *ATS*, p. 31).

Newman, Erasmus and an icon of Christ

We will conclude this overview of de Lubac's life with two entries from the diaries of the French author Julien Green,[6] who, although only four years younger than the theologian, met him in person for the first time in May 1978 and very soon came to hold him in high esteem. For his part, de Lubac admitted that he liked to read Green's books. Green, whose turbulent life story included two conversions to the Catholic faith (the first in 1915 and the second, after an intervening Buddhist phase, in 1939), recorded his impressions. The entry dated May 16, 1978, reads: "A few days ago [I paid] a visit to Fr. de Lubac, with whom I was not acquainted and who welcomed me with charming courtesy into his small room on the fifth floor of a modern building in the Rue de Sèvres.

---

[6] Julien Green (1900–1998) was a French writer; his diaries from the years 1926 to 1990 were published in five volumes [each entitled *Journal* with a subtitle] (1991–1995), in French and German editions; the citation is from vol. 4 of the German edition (1994).

Books lined the walls, but fewer than I would have expected. Slim, dressed in black, with fine features, eyes of a beautiful shade of blue and charmingly expressive, which radiate a subdued and peaceful strength. He told me how much he admired Newman." [7]

Green felt that this first conversation was still a bit halting, but he took his leave, hoping that they would meet again. Numerous conversations followed. Here is just an excerpt from the diary entry dated November 20, 1978:

> Toward late afternoon I looked up Father de Lubac. I found him in the tiny room in which he works. A little weary at first, but enchantingly cordial . . . in this very simple décor consisting of books, among which I noticed the reproduction of a marvelous Russian icon of Christ, and further down, leaning against the books, a portrait of Erasmus. [8] Then, when he spoke about the Council, the priest suddenly and positively blossomed and was extraordinarily rejuvenated. This tall old man dressed in black with the narrow face beamed with spirituality. . . . He told me that he knew the Council, since he had collaborated with the conciliar commission, and that the legend about the Council which has become established in public opinion by no means corresponds to the reality. What has been called the Rhineland group [which

[7] John Henry Newman (1801–1890) was an English theologian and founder of an Oratory (a priestly association). In 1845, he converted from the Anglican to the Catholic Church. He was created a cardinal in 1879. His *Essay on the Development of Christian Doctrine* (1845) was a pioneer work leading to a theory about the development of doctrine. His sermons especially are well worth reading.

[8] Erasmus von Rotterdam (1466–1536) was the most important Christian humanist [of the Renaissance period]. Among his other accomplishments was the first critical edition of the New Testament. He denounced abuses in the Church before Luther did, although he did not share the latter's views on justification, which he attacked in his 1524 work, *De libero arbitrio* [On free will].

probably refers to Cardinal Frings, Archbishop of Cologne, and his *peritus* Joseph Ratzinger, among others] actually was made up of outstanding theologians. Confusion prevailed only in the postconciliar activities. France never sent a serious journalist to the Council; they were always on the lookout merely for the *bon mot* or the anecdote, things suited to providing the public with picturesque details. Later he added that in today's world prayer has been eclipsed by action, as if it were not something different from action. He expected much of John Paul II, whom he knew well and whose energy and prudence he respected. "The Church is stirring," he told me, "but she has always stirred."

PART TWO

THEOLOGY IN HISTORY

Paradox and Mystery

Henri de Lubac left no masterpiece of systematic theology, no comprehensive summa of his thought. His work is both many-faceted and versatile. His writings do not carry out a long, preconceived plan. He himself says, rather, that almost all of his writings were produced in response to unforeseen circumstances. "I have never claimed to be doing the work of philosophical systematization or of theological synthesis. That is not out of contempt on my part, quite the contrary. . . . [My purpose, rather, is to call to mind] in a more general way the great Tradition of the Church, understood as the experience of all Christian centuries, coming to enlighten, orient, expand our poor little individual experience, to protect us from aberrations, to open it to the paths of the future" (*ASC*, pp. 144–45).

Only a "Historian of Theology"?

At any rate we should not let this label and other modest self-characterizations of de Lubac fool us. It is true that many of his works are historical treatments of terminology—for instance, when, like a private investigator, he tracks down the associations of the adjectives "mystical" and "real" with the Latin term *corpus*,[1] or when he pursues the question of an

---

[1] See above, pp. 53–54, and also below, pp. 179–80.

alleged twofold final destination of man and tries to find the switching points where the theory departs from previous Tradition. All this "conceptual archaeology", however, is based on a theological insight that guides the academic research, so that the history of theology serves the pursuit of theological truth.

Synthetic Thinking

De Lubac's work also resists classification in a specific theological area. While it is true that during the 1930s de Lubac held a professorship in fundamental theology and the history of religion and occasionally gave a few lectures in dogmatic theology as a substitute instructor, he cannot be described as a specialist in the usual sense. His choice of what questions to take up and the manner in which he approached his themes, if not really new, was nonetheless unusual and original. His contributions are among the standard works in the most varied fields of research. In patrology, his work on Origen's understanding of Scripture is considered a classic. In medieval theology, his interpretation of Saint Thomas' doctrine on the final destination of man met with wide acclaim. And the great scholar of medieval exegesis Beryl Smalley admitted in 1983 that de Lubac's studies had to a great extent made her standard work obsolete.[2] More recent interpreters of the Italian Renaissance philosopher Pico della Mirandola agree with the perspective developed by de Lubac, which reads Pico not as a syncretist, but rather as a Christian humanist who is deeply rooted in the tradition of patristic theology and is attempting, from a position at the very heart of the Christian faith, to formulate a comprehensive view of the world

[2] Beryl Smalley, *The Study of the Bible in the Middle Ages* (1952), foreword to the third edition (1983).

and history. Finally, in the field of dogmatics, de Lubac has had a decisive influence, both in the theology of grace (and accordingly in theological anthropology) and also in ecclesiology, the doctrine about the Church.

De Lubac's thinking is highly synthetic and thus aimed at a synoptic presentation, and it thereby counteracts the tendency in recent theology toward increasing specialization and compartmentalization.

If one nevertheless insists on assigning de Lubac to a particular theological department, then we will have to call him a fundamental theologian. As he himself says, his sole passion is to defend the faith of the Church, not by an attitude of warding off challenges, but rather by an approach that tries to win over non-believers, build bridges and dismantle obstacles. Many of de Lubac's studies become misleading or must be considered as incomplete if they are regarded as dogmatic treatises, which they have no intention of being. He is convinced that the faith shines forth by itself and possesses a persuasive power, if only it is really itself and is not presented or lived out in a distorted form.

> Before it can be adapted in its presentation to the modern generation, Christianity in all necessity must, in its essence, be itself. And once it is itself, it is close to being adapted. For it is of its essence to be living and always of the time.
>
> The big task consists then in rediscovering Christianity in its plenitude and in its purity. A task which is always and ceaselessly called for, just as the work of reform inside the Church itself is called for always and ceaselessly. For even though Christianity is eternal, we are never once and for all identified with its eternity. By a natural leaning we never cease losing it. Like God Himself, it is always there, present in its entirety, but it is we who are always more or less absent from it. It escapes us in the very measure that we believe we

possess it. Habit and routine have an unbelievable power to waste and destroy.

But how should we rediscover Christianity if not by going back to its sources, trying to recapture it in its periods of explosive vitality? How should we rediscover the meaning of so many doctrines and institutions which always tend toward dead abstraction and formalism in us, if not by trying to touch anew the creative thought that achieved them? How many explorations into distant history such a research supposes! How many painful reconstructions, themselves preceded by long preliminary work! In a word, how much "archaeology"! The task is not for everyone, obviously, but it is indispensable that it be done and forever done again. Let us not think that it is possible to reach the goal cheaply: to try that would be a kind of fraud, and when it comes to essential goods, the crook is never successful.

It took forty years in the desert to enter into the Promised Land. It sometimes takes a lot of arid archaeology to make the fountains of living water well forth anew.[3]

"I Will Never Write My Most Important Book"

Henri de Lubac not only wrote no systematic masterpiece—he even admits that he never wrote his most important book. In 1956, he noted: "I truly believe that for a rather long time the idea for my book on Mysticism has been my inspiration in everything. I form my judgments on the basis of it, it provides me with the means to classify my ideas in proportion to it. But I will not write this book. It is in all ways beyond my physical, intellectual, spiritual strength. I have a clear vision of how it is linked together [i.e., its thematic subdivisions] . . . , [but] the center always eludes me" (*ASC*, p. 113).

[3] *Paradoxes of Faith* (San Francisco: Ignatius Press, 1987), pp. 57–58; here cited as *PF*.

Connected with this is a further characteristic of his theological style. Just as the individual fields of specialization must be brought together in a perspective of theology's point of unity, so too for de Lubac the unity of life and doctrine, of theology and spirituality, is central. He sought to overcome not only the division between philosophy and theology, but also the division that already in the Middle Ages was becoming evident in the field of theology itself, namely, the division between spirituality and theology. Just as he expected a conversion in his students at the beginning of their studies (see above, p. 49), just as he himself did not allow his personal troubles and many unjustified suspicions and enmities to drive him into antagonism toward the Church and the competent superiors of his Order, but rather saw in the sorrow that befell him a form of taking up his cross and following Christ, so too for him theology was first and foremost an existential task. The mystery (see below, pp. 115ff.) that the theologian encounters and reflects upon is at the same time an example, a model and a norm by which to live. The Christ event, which renews everything, draws the theologian who approaches it thoughtfully and studiously into a process of renewal as well.

". . . Chosen on Account of Their Beauty"

By way of introduction, we should also point out a hurdle that sometimes stands in the way of reading de Lubac's works. The reader who does not have at least a basic knowledge of Latin may become discouraged after a few pages while reading some (but certainly not all) of de Lubac's works, because he is confronted again and again with extensive Latin citations. He remarked in the interview *Entretien autour de Vatican II*, "Several people have reproached me in a friendly way for not translating most of the citations. That may have been due to laziness, but also because many of these passages were chosen on account of their beauty, which a translation would have spoiled" (p. 89). The new edition of *Surnaturel* (1991) includes for the first time a translation of all the citations in an appendix, and so it is also in the new edition of the complete works (since 1998).

A Passion for Theology

An initial conclusion from what has been said thus far might read: de Lubac is not primarily concerned with teaching from a theological manual; if you are looking for a textbook, he will not be much help. Anyone who gets involved with him will learn instead how to think theologically. He will encounter a fascinating theological style, a passion for coming to know the truth as it makes its way through history. The hallmark of this style is his overwhelming knowledge of the history of theology and his familiarity with all the important thinkers of the most diverse epochs. The fact that he consistently deals with the sources themselves and is suspicious of too much secondary literature is an expression of this passion. "In his astonishing (but characteristic) way he scatters throughout the text the treasures of his inexhaustible memory—the accomplishment of all generations, stored up in fullness, yet with composure"—thus has Michel Sales[4] described de Lubac's manner of presenting his materials. Ignatius of Loyola, in his *Spiritual Exercises*, directs us to find God in all things and, as far as possible, to meet an author or a conversation partner halfway. De Lubac's style appears to be the consistent application of Ignatian spirituality to the work of theology.

[4] Michel Sales, *Der Mensch und die Gottesidee* (1978), p. 28.

History as the Place for the Encounter with God

The term historicity can be understood in two ways. There is an interest in history that sees in the historical development of ideas only their relativity; everything has become historical, "merely historical". De Lubac rejects this understanding, which can be traced back to deism.[5] According to the Christian understanding, history is the place for the encounter with the God who reveals himself. History is neither an expression of relativity, nor so much ballast standing in the way of immediate contact with God. "God acts in history and reveals himself through history. Or rather, God inserts himself in history and so bestows on it a 'religious consecration' which compels us to treat it with due respect" (*Cath*, p. 165). We must go even a step further. Christianity, as the religion that is conscious of being founded upon God's biblically attested self-revelation, not only takes history seriously, but is in the final analysis the religion that brought about historical thinking in the first place. A comparison with nonbiblical religions shows also that Christianity alone recognizes that history has a direction and purpose and thus does not result in a flight from the world and from history, but rather leads to a shaping of the world and of history (*Cath*, pp. 142–43).

Against this background, then, the history of dogma is also the place in which the testimony of historical revelation is handed on under the circumstances of human language and culture. *The witness to and assimilation of historical revelation necessarily must itself have a historical character.* That is the basis for de Lubac's passion for the history of theology. In comparing the theology of the Church Fathers with certain currents in modern scholarship in the history of religion, de Lubac

---

[5] About deism, see p. 34, n. 12, and p. 161, n. 1.

observes a peculiar reversal. Whereas the early theologians had and could have, in comparison with us, only a rudimentary knowledge of historical developments, they nevertheless had a distinct awareness of the uniqueness of God's self-communication within that same history. Our age, in contrast, possesses a vastly better knowledge of historical details and can trace individual lines of development, but, on the other hand, it has lost that understanding of history as the place in which God is revealed. This [shortsightedness] should be rejected, especially when it is a question of theological interpretations. De Lubac cites the words of Theo Preiss, who had written about the originality of the Christian interpretation of Scripture:

> However strange it may seem to us today, this exegesis as it was practiced by the first Christian generations, it nevertheless distinguished itself by its understanding of history from the sort [of textual interpretation] carried on in the Hellenistic milieu. . . . In a world that regarded history as something quite foreign, this exegesis—fantastic as it may have been in its details—still defended precisely this sense of history. Nowadays, in the name of history, we often equate such exegesis with a form of mythological thinking, which shows a certain lack of understanding and in fact does little credit to our sense of history.[6]

The Many Mysteries and the One Mystery

According to the Neo-Scholastic understanding, God's revelation consists primarily in a communication of truths about God that are inaccessible and also incomprehensible to man's unaided reason. The science of theology takes these revealed

---

[6] Henri de Lubac, *Typologie, Allegorie, Geistiger Sinn*, trans. Rudolf Voderholzer (Einsiedeln: Johannes Verlag, 1999), p. 391.

propositions (articles of faith, dogmas) as the point of departure for a deductive process in which the divine reality is investigated in greater depth.

This understanding of theology had developed in the age of Scholasticism, when the theory of science proposed by the Greek philosopher Aristotle was adopted, which defined science as a method of gaining well-founded knowledge, starting from first principles that are no longer demonstrable. In contrast to this view, which described the divine mystery entirely within the reach of human reason and on the level of rational deductive thought, the Tübingen School in the nineteenth and early twentieth centuries had developed a so-called theology of mystery, which harked back to the biblical and patristic[7] understanding of *mysterium* [Greek *mystérion*].

According to this approach, prior to all legitimate and necessary differentiation into the mysteries of the faith, formulated as propositions, God himself is the one inexhaustible Mystery, who in Jesus Christ has revealed the mystery of his will, that is, of his plan of salvation (see Eph 1:9). This self-disclosure, which aims at establishing communion between God and mankind, is a profoundly personal event. Every personal communication, for instance, a declaration of love, is ultimately based on the free-will decision of a person and thus remains incomprehensible in its depths, even when it is expressed to someone. Similarly, the revelation of God does not do away with the mysterious character of the Trinity of Divine Persons; even though he reveals himself and is near, God is and remains the incomprehensible Mystery. Against this background, theology is not so much a deductive process for acquiring deeper understanding as it is a subsequent reception of this divine self-revelation in Jesus Christ—a

---

[7] "Patristic" is a term from the history of theology referring to the time of the Church Fathers (until about A.D. 750).

response made possible by the Holy Spirit. *Non est enim aliud Dei mysterium nisi Christus* (There is no other mystery of God besides Christ), said Saint Augustine (*Epistula* 187, 34), who is cited by de Lubac. In Christ, God has revealed himself to mankind. Faith is the response to this communication. Thus in Christ all of dogma is contained as well.

> Under its form of action and under its form of revelation, as reality and as the object of faith, this unique and total Thing carries one and the same name in Scripture and in Christian Tradition: it is *mystery*. It is already a first abstraction, therefore, to separate completely the gift and the revelation of the gift, the redemptive action and the knowledge of redemption, the mystery as act and the mystery as proposed to faith. It is a second abstraction to separate from this total revelation or this "Whole of Dogma" certain particular truths, enunciated in separate propositions, which will concern respectively the Trinity, the incarnate Word, baptism, grace, and so on.[8]

According to de Lubac, these abstractions are legitimate and necessary, for the human mind grasps a complex reality only by differentiating and subdividing. Theology must take care, however, that the original coherence is not lost, that the connection of all the dogmas with their one origin is preserved and that no one succumbs to the erroneous opinion that the *mysterium* can be expressed exhaustively in a rationalistic manner.

In connection with the *mysterium* of the Church, de Lubac describes what *mysterium* means in the Christian dispensation:

> First, the mystery is somehow linked to God's design for man, whether as marking the limit of or the means of realizing this destiny. It is not, therefore, something irrational or

---

[8] Henri de Lubac, "The Problem of the Development of Dogma", in *Theology in History*, trans. Anne Englund Nash (San Francisco: Ignatius Press, 1996), p. 274.

absurd or merely non-contradictory; but, even so, the intellectual approach will always be fruitless, we are dealing with something that defies analysis, a smooth partition-wall, as it were, that one can hurl oneself against but not get a grip on. Neither is it a truth which would remain provisionally out of reach but as human reason attained "adulthood" would become progressively more accessible, as man narrowed down the mystery to manageable proportions. . . . The Church is a mystery for all time out of man's grasp because, qualitatively, it is totally removed from all other objects of man's knowledge that might be mentioned. And yet, at the same time, it concerns us, teaches us, acts in us, reveals us to ourselves. . . . The visible revelation par excellence of mystery is, therefore, the life of Christ. . . . The actions of Christ are genuinely human actions, set in history; but being also the actions of a divine Person, in each of them God becomes humanly visible and tangible. To understand the meaning of Christ's life is to penetrate into the divine reality (*CPM*, pp. 13–14).

His Thought-Pattern: The Paradox

Closely connected with the concept of *mysterium* in the writings of de Lubac is his discussion of *paradox*. Max Seckler declares, "His thought-pattern is the paradox." [9] For de Lubac, all mysteries of the faith have a *paradoxical* structure as tenets developing from the one original *mysterium*.

This should be explained more clearly so as to avoid misunderstandings. A *paradoxon* (Greek *para*, "against", and *doxa*, "opinion" or "expectation"), since the age of classical Greek philosophy, has meant a "strange", "surprising" or "shocking" statement. The term also appears in the New

---

[9] Max Seckler, "Die scholastische *'potentia oboedientialis'* bei Karl Rahner und Henri de Lubac", in M. Thurner, ed., *Die Einheit der Person*, Festschrift for Richard Heinzmann (1998), p. 314.

Testament: Luke 5:26 describes the reaction of the people to the healing of a lame man. They are beside themselves and say, "Today we have seen *paradoxa*!" The ecumenical German translation settled on "something *unbelievable*". The Vulgate Latin says *mirabilia* (wonderful things). Based on this usage, the term makes its way into patristic theology.

Later on, Pascal, Kierkegaard and Newman return to the deeper, biblical significance of *paradox*, and this is also the point of departure for de Lubac's use of the term. "The whole of dogma is thus but a series of paradoxes, disconcerting to natural reason and requiring not an impossible proof but reflective justification. For if the mind must submit to what is incomprehensible, it cannot admit what is unintelligible" (*Cath*, p. 327). *Paradox*, then, does not mean a riddle, or something nonsensical; rather, it denotes the "demands" of faith, that the believer should combine in thought certain realities that are clearly not mutually exclusive, even though finite human reason often cannot see how these things can be reconciled with one another. De Lubac mentions further examples: "God creates the world for his own glory, *propter seipsum*, and yet out of pure goodness; man is capable of action and free, and yet he can do nothing without grace, and grace works in him 'both to will and to perform' [see Phil 2:13]; the vision of God[10] is a free gift, and yet the desire of it is at the very root of every soul" (*Cath*, p. 327).

It is a similar situation with the Church, which is a visibly constituted society that is nevertheless invisible as well. Or with Mary, who is at the same time Virgin and Mother. Or with Christ, who is both true God and true man.

---

[10] The beatific vision (*visio beatifica*) refers to the fellowship with God that Christ made possible again. This sight of God is promised to man after his death and will fulfill all his longings.

[T]he idea of a God-Man is itself something that hits the mind head-on; even though we can see that there is no contradiction within the idea, the whole chain of realities associated therewith creates a mental atmosphere of bewilderment. Stop to think for a moment: "He who is the Power and Wisdom of God himself, and in whom all things visible and invisible were created, was, we are to believe, narrowly circumscribed within the limitation of that Man who once appeared in Judaea—entered into the womb of a woman, was born a baby, crying as the newly born always cry! . . ." [Origen]. And the mention of the cross completes the mental checkmate. A God "born and crucified" [Justin Martyr]!—it is "a sacredly terrifying mystery!" "Unto the Jews indeed a stumbling block, and unto the Gentiles foolishness" [1 Cor 1:23]. . . . If we no longer experience the shock of the statement, may not the reason be that our faith has lost its cutting edge, however honest or firm it may be, and probably is? Its object has had the *mana* taken out of it, and habit has made us comfortable so that neither in prayer nor in the business of living are we able to achieve compassion, in its strict sense, any longer (*SpCh*, pp. 48–49).

Human reason is tempted to impatience with the tensions inherent in these paradoxical statements and tends to resolve the polarity in favor of one of the two terms. In this regard we could formulate a definition of heresy:[11] a retreat into the notion of "nothing but", a truncation of the complex form of the *mysterium* to something more easily grasped by man's "trivial" understanding, and saying, "No more than this!" Christ: only a man. Mary: only a mother. The Church: only an invisible reality.

Applied to the concept of *dogma*, this leads to the insight: dogma is the act of keeping Catholic truth open and the

[11] The word *heresy* (Greek *hairesis*, "separation"), in theology, refers to a statement that contradicts dogma.

rejection of one-sided, reductive interpretations (for instance, "Christ was nothing more than a man") by acknowledging that he was fully God and fully man. As opposed to a popular understanding of dogma as a restriction of thought that sets a partial truth in concrete, it thus becomes clear that, on the contrary, dogma in the Christian sense represents the rejection of reductive interpretations and the freeing and broadening of the mind to apprehend the surprisingly new mystery that no man could have devised. This sort of paradox has nothing to do with self-contradiction, absurdity or "squaring the circle" (as Spinoza characterized the dogma of the union of God and man in Jesus Christ).

For de Lubac, this is the hallmark of what is specifically "Catholic", as distinguished from what is "Protestant": whereas the latter often ends up in "Either–Or" oppositions, the Catholic understanding is thus: Scripture *and* Tradition, authority *and* freedom, faith *and* works, and so on (see *MS*, p. 219).

One of de Lubac's chief concerns, running through all his writings, is to reunite things that belong together but have been torn apart and to expose false alternatives. Karl Heinz Neufeld remarks, "All of de Lubac's theological work illustrates his effort to overcome a dualism and extrinsicism that artificially tears reality apart." [12]

To someone who surveys de Lubac's voluminous work, it can easily appear, as Hans Urs von Balthasar put it, that he is facing an impenetrable jungle. But once the reader has become sufficiently well acquainted with this work, he recognizes that everything ultimately proceeds from one fundamental intuition and constitutes an organic whole.

[12] Karl H. Neufeld, "Öffnung und Freiheit: Zum 90. Geburtstag von Kardinal Henri de Lubac, S.J.", *Zeitschrift für Theologie und Kirche* 108 (1986): 321.

In the following sections we will illustrate this with reference to several of the central theological themes in de Lubac's writings. Again and again we will let him speak by means of substantial quotations, so as to convey something of his "theological poetry" as well. Last, but not least, this study should make clear how much de Lubac did to prepare for Vatican II and, accordingly, how he should also be considered as one of its authentic interpreters.

Man in the Presence of God

Impetus from Maurice Blondel

> Yes or no, does human life make sense, and does man have a destiny? I act, but without even knowing what action is, without having wished to live, without knowing exactly either who I am or even if I am. This appearance of being which flutters about within me, these light and evanescent actions of a shadow, bear in them, I am told, an eternally weighty responsibility, and that, even at the price of blood, I cannot buy nothingness because for me it is no longer. Supposedly, then, I am condemned to life, condemned to death, condemned to eternity! Why and by what right, if I did not know it and did not will it? [1]

With these words begins a book that opened the doors to an academic career for its author (see above, p. 35) and made theological history: Maurice Blondel's *L'Action*, published in 1893. *L'Action*, a word that is difficult to translate, in any case means more than "deed"; a more comprehensive equivalent is "actualization". Blondel wants to get to the bottom of this actualization and the concomitant human determinants and ramifications that are expressed therein.

> I shall make a clean breast of it. If there is something to be seen, I need to see it. Perhaps I will learn whether or not this

[1] Maurice Blondel, *Action: Essay on a Critique of Life and a Science of Practice*, trans. Oliva Blanchette (Notre Dame, Ind.: University of Notre Dame Press, 1984), p. 3.

phantom I am to myself, with this universe I bear in my gaze, with science and its magic, with the strange dream of consciousness, has any solidity. I shall no doubt discover what is hidden in my acts, at that very depth where, without myself, in spite of myself, I undergo being and become attached to it (*Action*, p. 3).

Presenting this doctoral dissertation was a missionary act. The faculty to which Blondel submitted it was the philosophy faculty of the anti-clerical Sorbonne, in Paris. Here the intellectual elite in France prepared for their teaching careers. And they insisted on independence from religion and the Church. *Séparation!* Philosophy is sufficient unto itself and rejects any claim by theology.

For a long time, Blondel thought that he was called to be a priest. After an intense interior struggle recorded in his published diaries and with the support of his confessor, he finally recognized that his "mission field" was to be the world of philosophy, which had cut itself off entirely from faith and the Church. His goal was to bring the young people who studied at the Sorbonne, and whose worldview would leave its mark on spirituality in France, closer to the Christian faith. For ten years, he worked at his first *opus*, in which he attempted as a philosopher, using strictly philosophical methods—that is, without relying on the truths of revelation—to prove that a worldview that closes itself off from God is unsatisfactory. *L'Action* is also a masterpiece of the lay apostolate.

Absolutely Unattainable and Absolutely Necessary: The Supernatural

"What does a person will when he really wills everything that he wills?" This question drives the analysis of the dynamic actualization of man at every level, and the result is that the

spiritual and volitional human dynamic of striving aims beyond any fulfillment that would be possible within this world.
Man does not only *have* a longing for the absolute, his very
existence *is* this longing. After more than four hundred pages
of razor-sharp reflections, Blondel sums up: "There is in man
a life better than man, and it is not man who can sustain life;
something divine has to dwell in him. *Absolutely impossible and
absolutely necessary for man: that is properly the notion of the
supernatural.* Man's action goes beyond man; and all the effort
of his reason is to see that he cannot, that he must not restrict
himself to it" (ibid., p. 357).

In a concluding chapter, Blondel juxtaposes the answer of
faith with the question that man is to himself. He demonstrates that through the Gospel message about the Incarnation, death and Resurrection of Jesus Christ and the abiding
presence of the absolute in the Sacraments, and in the call to
take up one's cross and follow Christ, the fulfillment of the
deepest demands of man's intellect and will is offered, together with the purification, refinement and liberation of
these faculties.

> To go to the end of the determinism of the exigencies of
> human action and of the chain of the relations necessary for
> the completion of our destiny, then, God has to offer Himself
> to us as if annihilated, so that we may restore to this apparent
> nothingness its fullness. In accordance with what we have to
> conceive and hope for, He makes Himself so small that we
> can hold Him, so weak that He needs us to lend Him our
> arms and our acts, so condescending [i.e., lowly] that He
> hands Himself over to the ebb and flow of sensible-life, so
> dispossessed that we have to return Him to Himself, so dead
> that we have to engender Him anew, as in the mysterious
> labor which brings forth living members from inert nourish-
> ment. It was the great temptation to become "like gods";

impossible dream. And yet man seems to have been given the ability to work a greater wonder: to be, we must, we can bring it about that God be for us and by us (ibid., pp. 386–87.)

The Sorbonne accepted the dissertation. Blondel went on to be a professor of philosophy in Aix-en-Provence. *L'Action*, however, became the manifesto of a Catholic renewal that began to free itself from intellectual isolation. As Tilliette puts it,[2] *L'Action* and the theology that it inspired were a veritable "release from imprisonment" for a whole generation of students, because the self-satisfaction of anti-clericalism was thereby convicted of its intellectual insufficiency.

Thus Blondel started to overcome the separation between philosophy and theology, between faith and the world, and this victory inspired "three philosophies that grew out of theology",[3] which are associated with the names of Pierre Rousselot, Joseph Maréchal and, yes, Henri de Lubac. The last-mentioned elaborated more completely and profoundly the philosophy of theology that Blondel had initiated.

Theological Elaboration

In 1932 de Lubac wrote in a letter to Blondel that it was the latter's book that had prompted him, more than eleven years previously, to reflect on these problems concerning the supernatural,

> . . . and I believe that I have remained faithful to its inspiration. If it were necessary to try to define it, I would willingly take as a formula this text from your *Itinéraire philosophique*

[2] Xavier Tilliette, "Henri de Lubac: Das theologische Vermächtnis", *Internationale Katholische Zeitschrift Communio* 22 (1993): 101.

[3] Peter Henrici, "On Mystery in Philosophy", *Communio International Catholic Review* 19, no. 3 (1992): 354–63.

[1928]: "There is a fear of mixing, confusing; there must be a fear of not uniting enough. . . . It is in fact when one does not know how to unite things well that one particularly fears confusing them. If the general life of humanity today too often withdraws from Christianity, it is perhaps because Christianity has too often been uprooted from the inner viscera of man (*ASC* p. 185).

In a later letter, de Lubac dispels Blondel's anxiety that he may not have followed the teaching of the Church on some point. Instead, he confirms Blondel's ideas from the theological perspective and says that the only regrettable thing is "that no theologian well enough aware of the total Tradition could be found to make everyone see that you are much more in the right than some of your most faithful disciples believe" (ibid, p. 187).

With regard to *L'Action*, de Lubac emphasized that Blondel is not concerned about the theological question of the beatific vision as the final destiny of man; rather, in purely philosophical terms, starting from an analysis of the volitional drive, he is studying man's duty to will, ultimately, what God wills, so as finally to want what he wants when he wants everything that he wants (see *MS*, p. 245). Yet Blondel's work also gave decisive impetus to the investigation of the theological question whether there can be a twofold final goal for man, or whether in light of biblical revelation there can ultimately be only one fulfillment for man, namely, life in and with God in the beatific vision of God as he is.

De Lubac would not and could not acquiesce in the notion current in Neo-Scholasticism that in order to preserve the freedom [i.e., gratuitous character] of God's grace, we must assume a *natura pura*, a sheer and unadorned human nature that can attain a sort of "natural blessedness" even without grace. For, so the argument went, an ordering to God alone as the one final goal would put God in man's debt, and man would have a right to the granting of this fulfillment, if God had created him that way in the first place.

First of all, the fatal error of this perspective can be seen in the fruits that it brought forth. The separation of philosophy from theology, indeed the refusal of reason to open itself to the Gospel message, could cite as corroboration the ground yielded within theology itself.

> They were dooming themselves to see [the supernatural order] as merely a kind of superstructure. It followed inevitably that man could not only have managed quite well without it, but that even now he could with impunity disregard it. It was deprived of any hold on human thinking or human existence. Christian thought was thus bounded by a narrow circle, in a quiet backwater of the intellectual universe, where it could only waste away. By the good offices of some of its own exponents, who were aiming to preserve its transcendence, it became merely an "exile".
>
> The price is heavy, but has the longed-for peace at least been gained by it? Far from it. Any repose of mind gained so easily can only be artificial. It does not express that harmony which can result only from overcoming opposition. Reason which has been suppressed will have its revenge all too soon by declaring that in such conditions the supernatural as presented to it, as forced upon it, is merely an illusion. . . . "[A] philosophy apart" and "a theology apart" [*théologie séparée*] are in strict correlation, both in history and in logic (*MS*, pp. 232–33).

De Lubac sets out from the fact that the idea of a natural perfectibility of man, in principle, is unknown in the Christian Tradition until the sixteenth century. *Ad te nos fecisti.* "Thou hast made us for Thyself, and our hearts are restless, O God, until they rest in Thee!" These words from the first lines of the *Confessions* of Saint Augustine, which de Lubac recalls over and over again, formulate this traditional understanding of faith in a way that is permanently valid. But how did the other theory come about?

What Led to the Theory of *Natura Pura*

There are many lines of development that converge in the sixteenth century and lead to the formulation of this theory. Tracing those strands and pointing out the decisive places in which they depart from Tradition is the main subject of the historical studies in *Surnaturel* (1946) and in the two volumes published in 1965 that take up this theme again: *Augustinianism and Modern Theology* and *The Mystery of the Supernatural*.

The catalyst, as so often in the history of doctrine, was the need to ward off a heretical teaching, but this led to a one-sidedness that in turn deviated from the true position. The stumbling block was the theologian Michael Bajus (1513–1589), who, in reacting to the Reformation, intended to align himself with Saint Augustine and his distinctive, well-defined theology of grace. "Everything is grace." That was Augustine's faith experience. But if this statement is understood, not as the expression of *existential* experience, but rather in an *ontological* sense,[4] then there is no room left for a relative autonomy of nature, for free will and decision making. Now, in fact, Augustine had not meant for his interpretation of grace to be taken in an ontological sense; at least this way of

---

[4] An *existential* experience refers to concrete human living, whereas the *ontological* meaning pertains to the philosophical or theological question as to the essence of things or the structure of being. For example, a Christian who has been (ontologically) sanctified through Baptism can experience himself (existentially) as a sinner.

framing the question was not his, since it was first formulated so explicitly in medieval philosophy and in the controversies of the Reformation. However, if one follows Bajus and Jansen (1585–1638) and confronts the Augustinian theology of grace with the question as it was framed in a later context, one distorts the theological anthropology of Augustine. With regard to this so-called Neo-Augustinianism of the sixteenth and seventeenth centuries, de Lubac speaks of mere pseudo-fidelity. Like Luther, Bajus collapses nature and grace together in such a way that the nature remaining after the loss of grace through original sin is little more than ungodly concupiscence. All works performed by pagans, however good and virtuous they may be, are sins, and their decisions are nothing but vices and lies. Everything that man does without grace is a mortal sin. This idea was condemned in 1567 by Pope Pius V, although the Magisterium did not base its ruling on a doctrine of *natura pura*. The theory of *natura pura* was never adopted by the Magisterium. It is unknown to orthodox theology as well. It was always only a theological opinion.

In contrast to this *anthropological pessimism*, Catholic theologians endeavored to formulate a more positive view of human nature: even fallen nature has retained a remnant of true freedom; unbaptized children who die are not automatically consigned to the torments of hell; the works of pagans are not necessarily sins (see *AMT*, p. 217). This anthropology, which was directed against Bajus, went on to combine with other trends in intellectual history.

The expression *natura pura* first appears in the fourteenth century. Within the framework of speculations about what God in his omnipotence (misunderstood here as arbitrary omnipotence) might have created, theologians invented a "pure nature", that is, a man who could find his perfection in something other than God. Yet this speculation was conscious of its own artificiality and thus confirmed once again the classical understanding, that God created man in his spiritual nature in such a way that he can attain his ultimate fulfillment and happiness only in God. Another strand of argument came from solutions to the question of what happens to unbaptized children who die, since they cannot simply be considered damned. Although they would not be perfected in the beatific vision of God, they still could attain a sort of natural blessedness, corresponding to the aspiration of their human nature.

Furthermore, the Renaissance and the rediscovery of antiquity, with its philosophy and its humanistic ideal, paved the way for a theology of pure nature. An important point of departure for this development is the work of Dionysius the Carthusian (d. 1471). On the basis of humanist notions of a natural religion and a pure philosophy, he explicitly contradicted Thomas Aquinas and maintained that the final end of man as the ancient philosophers had viewed it (*theoria*, "vision of ideas", knowledge of the truth) was in fact his natural end as well. Of course, Dionysius was aware of the fact that he was thus contradicting Thomas Aquinas, who had criticized the ancient philosophers precisely because they had not recognized man's final end, while at the same time excusing and pitying them, since they could not have recognized the true end of man before the revelation of Christ (see *AMT*, p. 126). Within half a century, though, a radical change took place: whereas Dionysius still realized that he was taking a stance against Thomas, Cajetan[5] presents this theory as an interpretation of Thomas himself.

Behind this development was a transformation in the

---

[5] St. Thomas Cajetan de Vio (1469–1534) was a Dominican friar and the most important theologian of the premodern period. From 1507 to 1522, he composed a complete commentary on the *Summa theologiae* of St. Thomas Aquinas. In 1518, he carried on a discussion with Martin Luther.

understanding of what is meant by the term *nature*. Basically, it is not a question of nature as that word is understood by the natural sciences, but rather of nature in the philosophical sense. Aristotle had taught that every nature has an end or goal, and that in principle it can reach that goal by the powers proper to this nature. "The striving of the nature cannot remain unfulfilled", so the axiom went. The star travels its course, the plant grows and bears fruit, the animal hunts and captures its prey, the eye is directed to the light and finds its light. Corresponding to the longing of a nature there is a fulfillment that is possible on the level of the nature. Thomas Aquinas adopted the natural philosophy of Aristotle. Granted, with regard to man, Saint Thomas determined that his nature was essentially different from all other natures: the nature of man consists in his being the image and likeness of God. Thus man is, by his very nature, destined for the vision of God. That is the one true and final end of man; he cannot attain this end, however, by his own powers (i.e., by the powers of his own nature), but can receive it only as a gift from God himself, who sanctifies and deifies human nature. Within the framework of Christian theology, nature becomes creation. Man especially stands in a particular relationship to the Creator by virtue of the fact that he is made in the image and likeness of God. This theological adaptation of the Aristotelian natural philosophy by Saint Thomas was no longer understood by Cajetan and many others after him (because of the changing meaning of "nature", as that term is used in the natural sciences). He interprets the texts of Saint Thomas without taking into account this broadening of the concept. Cajetan started with a human nature understood in the Aristotelian sense: one that would necessarily be able to find its fulfillment. Consequently, in order to safeguard the freedom of grace, he was forced to assume that man's longing for the vision of God is *not* an orientation to his final end that is inherent in human nature, but rather that this orientation must be added on to human nature by grace.

> Swiftly followed by two of his [Dominican confreres] Koellin and Javelli, [Cajetan] originated an explanation of the texts of St. Thomas which, in essentials, was to continue, with some slight shifts of emphasis, among many of the commentators of the *Summa* and theologians down to our own century. According to Cajetan, man can have a really natural desire only for an end which is connatural to him [i.e., that corresponds to his nature]; in speaking of a desire to see God face to face St. Thomas could only speak of the desire awakened in man as he is considered by the theologian, that is, he states clearly, in man actually raised up by God to a supernatural end and enlightened by a revelation (*AMT*, p. 127).

With Cajetan the switch has been thrown. The so-called Scholasticism of the Baroque period will ultimately continue along those same tracks, although there were also warnings and skeptical opinions, which de Lubac likewise cites. With Robert Bellarmine (1542–1621), the theory of *natura pura* is fully developed, even though in his spiritual writings, with happy inconsistency, he remains faithful to traditional Augustinianism. A major and decisive step was taken by the Spaniard Francisco Suarez (1548–1617). With him and his disciples, the new doctrine made a breakthrough. From then on one would rarely find opinions that recalled the original understandings of the great theologians of the patristic period and the Middle Ages. De Lubac cites as one example the spiritual works of Pierre de Bérulle.[6] The prevailing under-

---

[6] Pierre de Bérulle (1575–1629) was a cardinal and the proponent of a Christ-centered spirituality. See *Bérulle and the French School: Selected Writings*, ed. with intro. and notes by William M. Thompson, trans. Lowell M. Glendon (Mahwah, N.J.: Paulist Press, 1989).

standing, however, denies that human nature strives for the supernatural, so as to make room for the possibility of a purely natural end and to safeguard God's freedom in bestowing grace. If there were no natural blessedness, Suarez explains, then the supernatural end of man would be something owed to him (see *AMT*, pp. 201ff.).

But that was not the teaching of Augustine, Thomas Aquinas or Bonaventure, to mention only the preeminent proponents of a completely unambiguous tradition with regard to this question. "The soul is naturally capable of grace; since from its having been made to the likeness of God, it is fit to receive God by grace, as Augustine says."[7]

The Human Spirit: The Desire for God

The dignity and nobility of man consist in the fact that because of his spiritual nature he is endowed with a *desiderium naturale ad videndum Dei*, a natural desire to see God, to experience beatific fellowship with God. This is not just a matter of an indeterminate openness, in the sense of a purely formal and unspecific *potentia oboedientialis* (ability to obey), nor of a mere "nonrepugnance", which in principle would offer no resistance to grace. "We must understand that the desire for God is something absolute—the most absolute of all our desires." De Lubac goes still further by defining the created spirit as desire for God: *"L'esprit est . . . désir de Dieu"*.[8]

This divine first principle in man is not destroyed by the Fall. In this connection de Lubac refers to the distinction between *imago* and *similitudo* that is found already in the

---

[7] *"Eo ipso quod facta est ad imaginem Dei, capax est Dei per gratiam, ut Augustinus dixit"*: Thomas Aquinas, *Summa theologiae*, I-II, 113, 10.

[8] Henri de Lubac, *Surnaturel: Études historiques* (1946), p. 483.

writings of Irenaeus of Lyons, based on the Vulgate Latin version of Genesis 1:26 ("Let us make man to our image [*imaginem*] and likeness [*similitudinem*]"). Sin destroyed the likeness of God in man but not the more fundamental imaging of God. Man is by his very essence the image of God. His essence is determined by the soul, which in the theological tradition is described as the locus of the desire for God.

To put it in the words of one of the most eloquent in the "cloud of witnesses"[9] of the Christian Tradition, Gregory of Nyssa:

> O man, scorn not that which is admirable in you! You are a poor thing in your own eyes, but I would teach you that in reality you are a great thing! . . . Realize what you are! Consider your royal dignity! The heavens have not been made in God's image as you have, nor the moon, nor the sun, nor anything to be seen in creation. . . . Behold, of all that exists there is nothing that can contain your greatness.[10]

The Supernatural Existential

Karl Rahner, who like Henri de Lubac wanted to overcome "two-story thinking", suggested in connection with de Lubac's *Surnaturel* that we should speak about a *supernatural existential* in man. He took the term *existential* from the philosopher Martin Heidegger. It should be understood as a fundamental determinant that is given in human nature itself, for example, existence in time or the ability to speak. Just as being-in-the-world or language belong to man, so too, according to Rah-

---

[9] "Cloud of witnesses" is an image from the Letter to the Hebrews 12:1, which recalls the many Old Testament witnesses to the faith so as to encourage Christians. It is typical of de Lubac's method to cite as many texts as possible to support his statements.

[10] Gregory of Nyssa, *In Cantica*, hom. 2; cited from *DAH*, p. 20.

ner, does his orientation toward God belong to man. De Lubac saw in this nothing opposed to his own concern, although the adoption of Heidegger's terminology seemed to him unnecessary and the description of this *existential* as *supernatural* only shifted the problem. De Lubac is in complete agreement with Rahner's characterization of man as a *mysterium* that is ultimately not completely explicable to himself.

> Man is a mystery. He is so in his very essence, in his nature. Not because the infinite fullness of the mystery which touches him is actually in himself, for it is strictly inexhaustible, but because he is fundamentally a *pour-soi* [thing unto itself] purely in reference to that fullness. When we have said everything the mind can take in, everything definable that is to be said about ourselves, we have as yet said nothing, unless we have included in every statement the fact of our reference [*Verwiesenheit*, "orientation"] to the incomprehensible God; and that reference, and therefore our nature itself in the most fundamental sense, is not really understood at all unless we freely allow ourselves to be caught up by that incomprehensible God.[11]

To characterize this peculiarity of man, de Lubac prefers the term *paradox*.

The Paradox of Man

De Lubac vehemently argues against the attempt to reduce the paradox of man, as it has been preserved for so long in the Tradition of the Church, to one pole or the other and thus to mutilate the balanced teaching of the Church. "All tradition, in effect—taking the word in its widest sense—passing from St. Irenaeus, by way of St. Augustine and St. Thomas and

---

[11] Karl Rahner, *Schriften zur Theologie*, 3:47–60; cited in *MS*, p. 275.

St. Bonaventure, without distinction of school, presents us with the two affirmations at once, not in opposition but as a totality: man cannot live except by the vision of God—and that vision of God depends totally on God's good pleasure" (*MS*, p. 234). Even in a well-intentioned attempt to formulate more profound reasons for the second of these two statements, the first must not be abandoned. All too often, of course, theologians are burdened by an "impatient anxiety to eliminate every paradox from the human situation and arrive at a positive and clearly understandable result" (*MS*, p. 235). Nevertheless, these two statements must be allowed to stand side by side. It is important to ponder the paradox of man: God created man in his spiritual nature in such a way that man reaches further than everything that he finds [in creation] and steps beyond himself toward God (*self-transcendence*). God made man for himself, he unceasingly draws him to himself, he planted within his heart an insatiable desire for him. And yet God does not on that account owe man the grace of his self-communication; rather, this life is freely granted. And only as such can it be truly beatific for man. If it were owed to man, then it would cease being God's free gift in love. In the brief concluding chapter of *Surnaturel*, de Lubac had already replied to this objection:

> The spirit does not desire God as an animal desires its prey. It wants to have it as a gift. It does not strive to possess the infinite: it would like a freely granted communion with a personal being. Assuming, therefore, that he could simply grasp his highest good, which is impossible, then it would no longer be his good. Do some still insist on speaking about a "claim"? Then we would have to say that the spirit's only claim in this regard is to claim nothing. . . . It demands that God be free in making his offer, as he himself (in a completely different sense) demands to be free in accepting this

offer. He wants as little to do with a happiness that he would steal for himself as he does with a happiness that he would be forced to accept. Thus the perfectly gratuitous character of the divine gift appears as something requested by the creature, both for its own sake and for the sake of God's greatness (*Surnaturel*, pp. 483–84).

Henri de Lubac could note with satisfaction that not only did his historical-theological analyses prove to be correct, but the Second Vatican Council also, in its Pastoral Constitution *Gaudium et spes*, which deals chiefly with these anthropological questions, incorporated into its own teaching the doctrine of the *one* final end of man, namely, God. "All men are in fact called to one and the same destiny, which is divine" (*Gaudium et spes*, no. 22).

Anonymous Christianity?

If, however, man is already disposed toward God even before any endowment of grace through Christ, why then does he actually need the Gospel and the Church any more? De Lubac poses this question in the chapter "Salvation only through the Church", in *Catholicisme*. Here (already in 1938!) de Lubac marshals all the concepts that Karl Rahner would take up again later in his theory of *anonymous Christianity*. As soon as he has formulated the thought, de Lubac acknowledges the problematic nature of this concept, but he can demonstrate that the core of this thought is in agreement with Tradition. De Lubac rejects the most far-reaching interpretation of anonymous Christianity, [an implicit faith] that would be spread throughout the world and that through the proclamation of the Gospel would merely be converted into "explicit Christianity". As he sees it, two questions in this connection should be strictly separated: the question about the possibility that non-Christians can be saved (which is mainly individual and belongs to the subjective order) and the question about the relation of Christianity to the non-Christian religions, as well as their meaning and importance. The Church, with confidence in the universal salvific will of God, has always recognized the possibility of salvation for men who through no fault of their own know nothing about Christ and who live according to their conscience, and to that extent one could speak of "anonymous Christians". But no new theory is needed for that. In de Lubac's opinion, an understanding of "anonymous Christianity" that views all religions as having equal value and as being equally effective ways to salvation leads to the error of disregarding the "revolutionary novelty of the Christian message". The Gospel brings about a "conversion" and should transform man to the depths of his heart and ultimately conform him to Christ. The existential or experiential character of the faith is entirely directed to this purpose (see the conclusion of *CPM*).[12]

---

[12] See Hans Urs von Balthasar, *Cordula oder der Ernstfall* (1966); Eng.: *The Moment of Christian Witness*, trans. Richard Beckley (San Francisco: Ignatius Press, 1994). In the Afterword to the third edition (1967), von Balthasar writes that de Lubac's "illuminating distinction between 'anonymous Christians' and 'anonymous Christianity' does full justice to the exigencies of the present hour" (p. 152).

The Discovery of God

"To my believing friends, including those who believe that they do not believe." So reads the dedication that de Lubac placed at the beginning of the first two editions of his book *De la connaissance de Dieu* (1945, 1948). The book was revised and expanded several times and now is available in English under the title *The Discovery of God*. Together with *The Drama of Atheist Humanism* and the later study on Nietzsche, it contains de Lubac's most important reflections on the question of God. De Lubac did not intend to write a textbook on the subject. His concern, as the dedication already makes clear, is to lead people to the faith and to accompany them along the way of faith.

Can God's Existence Be Proved?

Catholic theology has always insisted that the knowledge of God does not first come to man through the historical revelation of the Word of God. In the Letter to the Romans, Paul writes that ever since the creation of the world, the invisible reality, eternal power and divinity of God the Creator can be recognized from the works of creation with the aid of reason (Rom 1:19–20). The proof of the existence of God takes its classical form in the *quinque viae*, the five ways, of Thomas Aquinas (*Summa theologiae* I, 2, 3), five arguments demonstrating that God exists. The first and simplest way concludes from the existence of movement that there is a final unmoved Mover, which is not just another link in this chain of movements, but rather their basis. And this is--as Thomas says at the conclusion of each of the five ways—what we call God. The First Vatican Council, citing Saint Paul, declared that God "can be known with certitude by the natural light of human reason from created things" (DH 3004 [Dogmatic Constitution concerning the Catholic Faith, chapter 2.1]).

Perhaps because of the aphoristic style of the presentation in *De la connaissance de Dieu* (pp. 35–66; see *DG*), de Lubac has been accused of bordering on agnosticism[1] (see *ASC*, p. 81). Yet de Lubac is by no means intent on abandoning the proof of the existence of God or promoting some sort of irrationalism—quite on the contrary. Together with the entire Tradition of Catholic theology, he means to uphold the capability of the human mind to know God. God is not merely a matter of opinion, with some people considering the idea that there is a God a good thing, and others not. The positions of acknowledging the existence of God and denying it have not reached a stalemate, leaving nothing but an arbitrary decision for one of the two possibilities. Belief in God can be supported by incisive reasoning. De Lubac regards the proofs for the existence of God as subsequent systematic expressions of an original, spontaneous recognition of God's presence.

The classical proofs (of Thomas Aquinas) for the existence of God are based on the principle of causality.[2] This very principle was limited by Kant to empirical reality—that which can be investigated by the natural sciences—so as to

---

[1] Agnosticism is a philosophical stance that considers God to be unknowable by human reason.

[2] The principle of causality can be stated succinctly as follows: *contingency* presupposes *something absolute*. In other words, it is a fundamental truth that, because some things are dependent on others for their existence, there must be a reality that is dependent upon nothing for its existence.

make it unsuitable for any transcendent application. De Lubac criticizes this restriction of reason to what is empirically observable. To recognize a limit means to be beyond this limit already. Causality is a principle of being and of thinking in general. Every critique of the causality principle, and thus of the proofs for the existence of God, must presuppose that very principle and thus deprives itself of its own foundation. The design for the proof of the existence of God is firmer than the hardest steel. "It is something more than one of reason's inventions: it is reason itself" (*DG*, p. 62).

On the other hand, in countering a critique of the proofs for the existence of God mainly from the Protestant side, which is suspicious of the danger of usurping what is God's ("intellectual justification by works"), de Lubac views it as downright positive that this proof simultaneously demands the free acknowledgment of what is proved. There is a danger of thinking that by means of such a proof one has "grasped" or thoroughly comprehended God, but de Lubac counters this by insisting that the philosophical teaching about God can lead ultimately only to a *negative theology*.

Negative Theology

Negative theology means that we can say about God only what he is *not*, but never who he is and what his nature is. At first, as Martin Lenk has demonstrated, de Lubac argued against a deficit of negative theology, but later on against an excess of it (Lenk, p. 192).

In opposition to a rationalistic, philosophical doctrine about God that claims to know even God's essence, de Lubac at first emphasized the uniqueness of the proofs for the existence of God. "[I]f the *proof* of God's existence, starting from the world, is to be valid, and if it is really to be a proof of *God*, it is not, strictly speaking, indispensable to know anything about the divine essence; on the contrary, it seems indispensable not to be able to know anything. For that is the only way in which one can know something about him as distinct from all else" (*DG*, p. 127). In this negation of all images of God, which emphasizes God's transcendence and radical dissimilarity from everything that is created, the biblical critique of the pagan worship of idols and the Greek philosophers' critique of anthropomorphic notions of God are in agreement.

And yet. Even the classical philosophical doctrine about God, which followed the three steps[3] of affirming (*via affirmationis*), denying (*via negationis*) and transcending (*via eminentiae*), was inspired from the outset, according to de Lubac, by the positive *via eminentiae*, which is inherent in the dynamic of the mind and reaches out to the absolute, and hence stands at the end of the three-step process in more than just a chronological sense. The No of negative theology is borne up by a deeper affirmation.

Accordingly, de Lubac later on is primarily concerned about overcoming a deficiency that he notes in the Thomistic tradition of handling the proofs for the existence of God. The necessary emphasis on the limits to our knowledge of God, he says, has favored a trend toward a negative theology that ultimately leads to agnosticism, which claims to be unable to know God any more in the first place. Yet in every act of knowing something that is, God is also known as the ultimate ground of being; in every positive act of the will, God is also

---

[3] There are three steps in this way of thinking about God. One can say something about God (affirmation). But there is no comparison with anything else (denial). Finally—and this is the mainspring of the whole process—the thinking is taken to a level beyond itself and is referred to the mystery of God (transcendence).

affirmed as the highest and ultimate good. De Lubac speaks about a proleptic element in the intellectual act by which man fulfills himself, namely, a dynamic element that reaches out [to the being that is the object of knowledge or volition]. And when he adds parenthetically that it has become conventional to talk about this as "unthematic" knowledge of God (see *ASC*, p. 81), then he is emphasizing here his agreement with Karl Rahner. The latter formulates it in different words:

> By grasping the objective reality of his everyday routine (in apprehension and comprehensive comprehension), he also accomplishes, as the prerequisite for the possibility of such apprehending comprehension, an unthematic, object-less outreach to an ungraspable, unique fullness of reality, which in its unity is at the same time the prerequisite for knowledge and for the (individual) thing known, and which is always affirmed as such (unthematic), even in the act that argues this thematically.[4]

Therefore de Lubac does not intend to let the traditional proofs for God's existence fade from view, but rather to make them more profound and more secure against the consequences of an exaggerated negative theology. "The mind did not set itself in motion, and its movement presupposes a direction; that is to say, a fixed point. What is without foundation or purpose is a description of the absurd. One cannot do without God" (*DG*, p. 63). Looking back on his work, de Lubac himself writes, "It seems more important to me today than ever to stress this, at a time when an undue inflation of 'negative theology' risks opening the way not only to agnosticism but to atheism" (*ASC*, p. 81).

Nevertheless, *negative theology* has lasting value. It keeps us from exchanging the living God for idols of our own making.

---

[4] Karl Rahner and Herbert Vorgrimler, *Kleines theologisches Wörterbuch*, 11th ed. (1978); see the entry "Gottesbeweis".

Herein lies one of the connections to de Lubac's concern with atheism. He says that, unwittingly and against his will, "the atheist is often the greatest help the believer can have" (*DG*, p. 188). Not because the atheist is perhaps the better Christian (as Ernst Bloch maintained), but rather because the atheistic critique compels faith to examine and purify its notion of God; in this regard it can be compared with salt, "that will prevent my idea of God from petrifying and so becoming false" (ibid.). Conversely, de Lubac shows that in every place where man refuses to acknowledge God, something else is set up as an absolute. Man cannot get around God.

Two proponents of modern atheistic humanism were of special interest to de Lubac: Pierre Joseph Proudhon (1809–1865) and Friedrich Nietzsche (1844–1900).

Proudhon and Christianity

Pierre Joseph Proudhon is numbered among the so-called "Early Socialists". In 1941–1942, de Lubac delivered a series of lectures about him, which he published as a book[5] immediately after the War. This study reveals a deep sympathy with a man whose name is connected with the awakening self-consciousness of the working class and their demand for social justice. Even though de Lubac rejects Proudhon's later rhetorical attacks and sharp criticism of the Church, he cannot help respecting him, especially since the attitude of broad sectors of the Church toward the momentous new social question in the nineteenth century was shameful.

As a contemporary of Karl Marx, Proudhon wrestled with the same problems, yet arrived at a different economic theory

---

[5] Henri de Lubac, *Proudhon et le Christianisme* (1945); trans. R. E. Scantlebury, *The Un-Marxian Socialist: A Study of Proudhon* (New York: Sheed & Ward, 1948).

concerning property. Private property as such is not the root of all evil, but rather the disproportion between private property and the income earned from it without working. In this regard, Proudhon was opposed to Marx, who mocked him not only because of his traditional understanding of marriage, but also because he professed that the idea of God is inescapable.

Proudhon's economic theories as well as his relationship with Christianity are intimately connected with his personal plight. As a twelve-year-old, while attending school thanks to financial assistance, he had to go to work in order to help feed his family. When he was seventeen, his father, a cooper who owned a business establishment, went bankrupt. Before the eager student could complete his education, the nineteen-year-old Proudhon had to invest all of his efforts in being a breadwinner: he took a job at a printing press where, among other books, a famous Latin edition of the Bible was published. From then on, Proudhon always kept a copy of this Bible with him. An autodidact, he taught himself biblical Hebrew besides. The letters of Scripture left a deep impression on his heart. At the age of twenty-three, he left the Church and decided to write against religion, at least against what theologians had made out of it, as de Lubac makes clear.

Proudhon acknowledges that the idea of God is universal. He is less impressed by the proofs for the existence of God than by the fact that all men have an idea of God. Something absolute is required, or else all knowledge falls into chaos and nihilism. But that by no means implies a positive acknowledgment of God. For on the practical level God must be opposed. Proudhon's atheism is an *anti-theism*: precisely because the idea of God is inescapable, God must be fought all the more vigorously. One of Proudhon's slogans reads: "God is evil! What do we owe him? War!" What was behind such embittered words? De Lubac tries to make them comprehensible without justifying them. What Proudhon opposed was not the God of biblical revelation, but rather the "myth of Providence", to which contemporary theologians had allowed him to degenerate. Proudhon was combating a notion of God that downright cheerfully proclaimed poverty and misery to be the work of Divine Providence, inasmuch as it affords the rich an opportunity for works of charity and the poor—a chance to practice patience in suffering. He declared war on the sort of God that justifies human miseries. Proudhon, "who does not have sufficient faith to protest in the name of God, whom he bears within his heart, accepts, at least for the time being, the caricature that is presented to him. Thus, practically speaking, he arrives at his anti-theism" (*Proudhon et le christianisme*, p. 207).

The guideline for his activism was the biblical concept of "justice", which he contrasts with a false "love of neighbor" that has been misunderstood in this way. In his view, justice had been betrayed by the theologians of his time. Proudhon repeatedly declared that he would cease all opposition to the Church if it would concede that this justice was on his side. Given his impression of the situation in his times, the religious problem is focused, as he sees it, on the attainment of justice. He is fascinated by the Person of Jesus, but considers him primarily a moralist and a social reformer who restores justice. Proudhon never realized that justice and love of neighbor are not contradictory; rather, charity fulfills justice as the New Testament fulfills the Old. In any case, Proudhon did not put man in God's place, as so many contemporary and later systems of atheistic humanism have done. Proudhon knew that salvation is not to be found in man. Even though social conditions drive him to extol the worldly value of social justice to a quasi-divine status, the ultimate questions still do not leave him in peace. "'Ever since I existed I have thought of God!' In this exclamation of Proudhon's—Marx jeered at him for dallying with the outworn idea of metaphysics—it is the whole of humanity which testifies to itself and which, even in its denials, demands the air without which it suffocates" (*Cath*, p. 360).

Proudhon's anti-theism, which for Christians presents not so much a denial of the idea of God as the purification thereof, should serve as a warning and a wake-up call to Christians. A yet more radical anti-theism is formulated in the philosophy of Friedrich Nietzsche, with which de Lubac had already dealt in *The Drama of Atheist Humanism*; a few years later he devoted to this subject an additional essay, "Nietzsche as Mystic".

Nietzsche and Christianity

Even more decisively than Proudhon, Nietzsche is an antitheist. In the name of life, Nietzsche battles against God, whom he regards as nothing but an "enemy of life". God must be killed. "[I]t is man who has to free himself, by an act of will. He must dare. Faith in God, especially as inculcated by Christianity, has served to tame man (*zähmen*): what is necessary is to raise (*züchten*) him (in the sense of improving the breed) by rooting out that faith, so as to enable him in the end to raise himself" (*DAH*, p. 46).

Nietzsche is not the first to speak about the death of God. Initially the expression belonged to the Christian theology of Good Friday. *"O grosse Not, Gott selbst ist tot"* [What a calamity, God himself is dead] is a verse in a Lutheran-Evangelical hymn, which Nietzsche knew and which Hegel also cites in his discourse on "the speculative Good Friday":

God must embrace death as the ultimate opposition in order to realize himself.

In writing about the dying or dead God, Arthur Schopenhauer and Heinrich Heine diagnose the spiritual situation of their time, which, by dismissing metaphysics, has also taken leave of God.

In Nietzsche's work, the rhetoric about the death of God acquires another, more radical tone: it is not a lament, nor a mere statement of fact. "It expresses a choice. 'Now,' says Nietzsche, 'it is our preference that decides against Christianity—not arguments.' It is an act. An act as definite and brutal as that of a murderer. For him 'the death of God is not merely a terrible fact, it is something willed by him.' If God is dead, he expressly adds, 'it is we who have killed him. . . . We are the assassins of God' " (*DAH*, pp. 49–50).

What is Nietzsche's ultimate objective, according to de Lubac, in writing about the murder of God in this way? As he interprets him, it is not enough to refer to the question that Nietzsche places on Zarathustra's lips: "If there were gods in existence, how could I endure not to be a god?" It is not only the supposed competition between God and man; Nietzsche, after all, cannot imagine how man's freedom could be anything but restricted if it is subordinate to God's freedom. Nietzsche is convinced that believing in God is convenient for man. He folds his hands and submits, instead of raising himself up to his true greatness. To some extent, God is always filling in the gaps for man, and he prevents him from daring to go boldly and fearlessly to the limits of his possibilities. Concealed within faith in God, according to Nietzsche, is a secret egotism, which needs God in order to satisfy its craving for pleasure. But in order for man to reach his fullest potential, he must liberate himself from God and dare to take this dangerous, laborious step. "God is dead, long live the

Overman [superman]!"⁶ Pangs of conscience and despair, the foreseeable consequences of this act, to which man will only gradually measure up, must be overcome by dint of the same effort. "Since there ceased to be a God, loneliness has become intolerable: the man who overtops the rest *must* set to work." De Lubac explains: "Henceforth inventing and creating is the task of the true philosopher." It is a matter of affirming the will to power; the man liberated from God must take his life entirely into his own hands. "I am alone, and I would have it so," says Zarathustra. "Alone with a clear sky and an open sea."⁷

De Lubac admits that there is something seductive about Nietzsche's thought. The visions from which Nietzsche's philosophy and other humanistic forms of atheism were born are not without greatness; in many respects they have put their finger on genuine sore spots. But did the world that nauseated Nietzsche really have the right to call itself Christian (*DAH*, p. 70)? Isn't the God that he talks about murdering a mere caricature of the God whom Christians worship? On the other hand, the first half of the twentieth century showed what a civilization is capable of, once it has renounced God. Confronted with the bleak contempt for mankind, the hatred and the wars caused by a mankind that has been "unchained" in this way (recall that the book was published in 1944!), de Lubac counters: "Atheistic humanism was bound to end in bankruptcy. Man is himself only because his face is illumined by a divine ray" (*DAH*, p. 67). It is just not true that God belittles man and diminishes his stature. On the contrary, God alone lifts man up to his true greatness; he

---

⁶ Friedrich Nietzsche, *Der Wille zur Macht* [*The Will to Power*], as cited in *DAH*, p. 56.

⁷ Friedrich Nietzsche, *Also sprach Zarathustra* [*Thus Spake Zarathustra*], cited in *DAH*, p. 58.

does not hamper his freedom but rather challenges it to the utmost; he does not cripple or pacify him, but rather calls him to apply all his gifts and talents to the task of shaping the world. Never is man greater than when he kneels down in the presence of God.

> For man, God is not only a norm that is imposed upon him and, by guiding him, lifts him up again: God is the Absolute upon which he rests, the Magnet that draws him, the Beyond that calls him, the Eternal that provides him with the only atmosphere in which he can breathe and, in some sort, that third dimension in which man finds his depth. If man takes himself as God, he can, for a time, cherish the illusion that he has raised and freed himself. But it is a fleeting exaltation! In reality, he has merely abased God, and it is not long before he finds that in doing so he has abased himself (*DAH*, pp. 67–68).

In his later essay, de Lubac once again returns to Nietzsche.

Nietzsche as Mystic

De Lubac tries to explain how the idea of the superman in Nietzsche goes together with the notion of the "eternal return of the same thing", which would appear to contradict it. Nietzsche became acquainted with this idea of eternal recurrence, namely, that the course of history repeats itself again and again in the same way, from the Greek philosophers, and in his own writings it becomes increasingly central to his thought. De Lubac refers in particular to two experiences that Nietzsche had, which came over him like a "revelation". After the first experience on the cliff at Surlej, near Sils-Maria, in Engadin, he was as though enraptured and transported to another world. "Early August 1881 in Sils-Maria: six thousand feet above sea-level and at a much higher elevation over all human concerns! The sun of knowledge once again stands at midday, and the serpent of eternity lies diminished in its light." Then, in February of 1883, Nietzsche had a "vision" in Rapallo, where he was spending the winter. From then on, the idea of the "Eternal Return" had definitively taken possession of him.

Isn't that a depressing prospect? Isn't this eternal recurrence sheer absurdity? Nietzsche seems, on the contrary, to have felt at first that the eternal return was a source of happiness. De Lubac suggests the following solution: when faced with the eternal cyclical movement, Nietzsche can either

> be carried away passively in an immense and desperate rotation, or, on the other hand, he can participate in the dominating force that thus moves the entire cosmos. . . . He can suffer the iron law of universal determinism, but he can, on the other hand, be himself this very law in freedom. In the first case, he is destroyed, in the second, he triumphs. There is no emptiness more horrible nor any plenitude more overflowing (*DAH*, p. 484).

As de Lubac interprets it, this ambiguity seems to have been clarified definitively for Nietzsche in Rapallo. Nietzsche gains the certainty that he is standing on the side of being and is not being carried away by eternal becoming. "He participates actively, freely in *fatum*. He even belongs to it" (*DAH*, p. 486). This was Nietzsche's experience, and de Lubac calls it a mystical experience. He is one with fate; in him coincide freedom and destiny, as they do in God. "Nietzsche feels in himself the Force that produces everything and that finds itself intact, unchanged, free and sovereign in each instant of universal becoming. For him, existence is a circle whose center really 'is everywhere'" (p. 485). Nietzsche knows that he is on the side of being. And thus the idea of the Overman and the idea of the Eternal Return coincide, and

the question posed at the outset is answered. "He knows that
he is the Overman, he whose lawless will engenders worlds"
(p. 486). "Like the other kingdom, indeed, more truly than
the other one, he is at once its revealer and its object, its
messenger and its god. 'Noon. The time of the shortest shade.
End of the longest error. Culminating point of humanity.
Incipit Zarathustra [Zarathustra begins]'" (p. 487, citing *Götzen-
dämmerung* [Twilight of the Idols]).

And thus, in Nietzsche, whose initial word was a No to
God, the absolute has nevertheless gained acceptance, albeit
in a downright tragically distorted form. It turned out that
pure negativity was an impossible dream. The Overman
could not build himself in an absolute void. . . . Thus the
Eternal Return is imperative as the indispensable substitute
for a dead god. It alone can seal up the stone of his tomb
(*DAH*, p. 496).

This experience of Nietzsche's, nevertheless, is constantly
endangered. De Lubac points out Nietzsche's abiding "jeal-
ousy" with regard to Jesus. His fundamental stance is not so
much one of affirmation as it is a defiant, resentful attitude of
resistance. Until his dying day, Nietzsche would feel that he
was being pursued by Jesus, and his own feelings toward him
would alternate between amazement and backbiting, between tenderness and sarcasm.

And after all, in his final years, until his nervous breakdown
in Turin in 1890, Nietzsche was anything but composed
and contented. Depression and satiety weighed him down.
"You can no longer endure it, your lordly destiny? Love it,
for you do not have choice."[8] He confided to his friend
Franz Overbeck in a letter that "the barrel of a gun is now

[8] Friedrich Nietzsche, *Reden, Gleichnisse, Bilder* [1882–1888], cited in *DAH*,
p. 504.

a source of relatively pleasant reflections" for him (*DAH*, p. 506). And de Lubac concludes by applying to Nietzsche himself a saying that the latter originally aimed at Christianity: "This mystic 'does not need anybody to refute him. He takes care of this task himself'."[9]

If someone wants to compare Nietzsche's "mysticism" with a form of non-Christian "spirituality", the most likely candidate is Buddhism. His notion of the Overman displays similarities with Buddha, the enlightened man, who "by a mysterious and total intuition [knows] not the secret of a Being, who does not exist, but the secret of universal becoming. 'I am not a man, I am not a god. Know that I am a Buddha.' Thus could Zarathustra speak" (*DAH*, p. 490).

The Encounter between Buddhism and the West

The above is the title of the second of the three volumes that Henri de Lubac wrote about Buddhism[10] in the early 1950s, after he was forbidden to publish theological books. It is not so much a theological examination of the subject (which is carried out in the other two volumes) as a history of the "discovery" of Buddhism by Western missionaries and Western philosophy and theology. In this context, de Lubac discusses two inadequate ways in which Buddhism has been categorized by Christian thinkers.

As early as in the Middle Ages, there were instances of monks arriving in the Far East by the land route and meeting Buddhists there. To many of the monks the Buddhists appeared to be like brethren, so similar to their own did the Buddhist way of life and spirituality seem. A more intensive

[9] Friedrich Nietzsche, *Menschliches, Allzumenschliches* [Human, all too human], cited in *DAH*, p. 509.
[10] Henri de Lubac, *La Recontre du bouddhisme et de l'occident* (1952).

encounter with Buddhism became possible only with the discovery of the sea route in the late fifteenth century.

So began the first period of the encounter between the West and Buddhism. Contact was made chiefly by the missionaries from the various religious orders, who after 1492 committed themselves to spreading the Gospel in the newly discovered lands, even to the ends of the earth. Whereas most of them took Buddhism to be a wayward daughter of Christianity, the Chinese saw in many Christian sermons merely a variant of Buddhism. All in all, a negative view of Buddhism prevailed, the most extreme form of which de Lubac calls *exclusivism*. This view denies that there is even the least element of truth in Buddhism.[11]

Whereas in the first period Westerners tended to be too dismissive, the second period is characterized by a view that was generally too positive. In the extreme case, according to de Lubac, this led to syncretism. In the nineteenth century this trend included also the proponents of so-called traditionalism, a theory that postulated an original revelation given to men at the very beginning of history, which was then handed on. They supposed that they could detect a trace of this original revelation in Buddhism as well. With its inclination to interpret all phenomena as comparable, indeed, as ultimately derived from one and the same source, syncretism does justice neither to Christianity nor to Buddhism. There is [in this theory] no higher vantage point from which the original unity of the various religions could be comprehended once again.

Beyond exclusivism and syncretism, de Lubac argues for an encounter that recognizes Buddhism in its distinctive fullness,

---

[11] During this period in which Buddhism was generally rejected, the Jesuit missionaries Francis Xavier (1506–1552) and Matteo Ricci (1552–1610) were exceptions, viewing it positively.

an approach that is motivated by the greatest respect for Buddha and his followers. Together with Romano Guardini,[12] de Lubac speaks of Buddha as the great challenge for Christianity: "This man constitutes a great mystery. He moves in a frightening, almost superhuman freedom; at the same time he displays a goodness that is as mighty as a cosmic force" (*La Rencontre du bouddhisme*, p. 284). Nevertheless, from the Christian perspective, even after recognizing all that is positive in Buddhism, one must finally admit the incompatibility of the two religions (pp. 261–85).

The reason for this is the Buddhist understanding of the world, which one must call *monistic*. By monism (Greek *monos*, "one", "only") we mean a fundamental philosophical attitude that regards every difference and every confrontation, including and especially the confrontation of I and Thou, as something provisional and inferior. Against this background, the experience of I and Thou, of I and the World, can only be interpreted as a condition to be overcome. One's relation to the absolute or the divine, accordingly, is perfected when the individual dissolves in the absolute.

In de Lubac's opinion, the meeting of religions and dialogue among them can take place meaningfully only on the level of basic human experiences. In the two-volume *Aspects du bouddhisme* (the second titled *Amida*), de Lubac compares Christianity and Buddhism under several points of view.

Love and Selflessness

At first glance, the Buddhist doctrine of selfless love appears deceptively similar to the Christian doctrine. It is based on

---

[12] Romano Guardini (1885–1968), a Catholic theologian and philosopher of religion, compared Buddha with Jesus in *The Lord*, trans., from the German, by Elinor Castendyk Briefs (Chicago: Regnery, 1954), pp. 305–6.

doing no harm, offering no resistance, and is developed in the basic attitudes of benevolence, for example, kindness, giving, willingness to offer corporeal and spiritual aid, as well as compassion. In Buddhist writings, these virtues are praised. Especially impressive is the selflessness and universality expressed in them. For these virtues are to be practiced without any expectation of reward or return. In many ways, the texts cited by de Lubac recall biblical directives, and they command deep respect. Yet upon closer inspection differences become evident. Since Buddhism is a monistic system, it ultimately recognizes no true contrast between I and Thou. The love that is to be practiced so selflessly has no real recipient. The gift of self to a Thou is not possible—only self-renunciation and subordination to and unification with totality. Ultimately, then, everything remains unreal; love has not been "made flesh". De Lubac views all the deficiencies, indeed, the "perversity" of Buddhism as being based on its lack of interpersonal mutuality.[13] The radical tendency to flee or sublimate reality leads finally to an indifference that ultimately views *samsara* (the chain of reincarnations that are supposed to lead to redemption) and *nirvana* (the end of the reincarnations, dissolving into the absolute) as being one and the same. Salvation, in the final analysis, "is the destruction of a mere prejudice; there is no one who is saved."[14]

Amida

The second volume of *Aspects du Bouddhisme* is also titled *Amida*, which is the Japanese abbreviation for *Amida Butsu*

---

[13] Henri de Lubac, *Aspects du Bouddhisme*, vol. 1 (Paris: Seuil, 1951), p. 53; English ed. trans. George Lamb, *Aspects of Buddhism* (New York: Sheed & Ward, 1954).

[14] Asanga, quoted in Hans Urs von Balthasar, *The Theology of Henri de Lubac: An Overview* (San Francisco: Ignatius Press, 1991), p. 57.

(the Buddha of immense light and life). Amida-Buddhism is one of the mainstream forms of Buddhism in Japan (the others being Zen-Buddhism and Lotus-Buddhism).

Amida is a mythical, that is, non-historical figure of light, which has either driven out or else assimilated other competing heavenly figures. The similarity to Christianity consists in the fact that Amida is a quasi-divine figure who graciously condescends to men and the fact that one makes to this figure a kind of vow, an act of self-dedication, which at first glance appears to be comparable to a trusting act of faith. Prayers of supplications are also made to Amida Buddha, and his help appears as a gracious gift. Can we find here, perhaps, the interpersonal dimension, the prerequisite for love and faith-filled self-giving that was missing until now? But upon more careful analysis this similarity, too, proves to be deceptive. Aside from the fact that Amida, unlike Jesus, is not a historical but a mythological figure, the meeting of persons remains merely provisional here as well. In the end, *samsara* and *nirvana* are again identical. "Amida succumbs to the temptation to identity [i.e., monism] found in all non-Christian mysticism".[15] And yet even in an objectively inadequate path of salvation, the omnipresent grace of Christ can be effective. "We have no right to think smugly that God has left himself without witnesses everywhere outside of Christianity." [16] At any rate, the mythological figure of Amida and the possibility of devotion to it in faith is, in principle, a sign of openness to a personal God.

If, as Guardini suggests (*The Lord*, pp. 305–6), Buddha can be called a forerunner of Jesus and can be numbered among

---

[15] Henri de Lubac, *Amida—Aspects du Bouddhisme*, vol. 2 (Paris: Seuil, 1955), p. 301; trans. George Lamb, *Aspects of Buddhism* (New York: Sheed & Ward, 1954).

[16] Ibid., p. 307.

the Old Testament figures who foreshadowed Jesus, then he most resembles Qoheleth, the author of the Book of Ecclesiastes. The latter's warning against deceptive appearances, his unmasking of all forms of idolatry, is in its own way a sort of negative theology. But herein lies, from a Christian perspective, a possible theological place for Buddha: "Through the exclusion of false ideas about God, Buddhism creates an empty space that can become openness to the true God" (Lenk, p. 242). What is hinted at in the figure of Amida has finally become reality and truth in Jesus Christ, who surpasses all prefigurations and foreshadowings

Jesus Christ: Word of God
and the Way to Men

De Lubac never produced a work on mysticism, even though he viewed Christian mysticism as the central inspiration for all of his thinking; similarly, he never wrote a book specifically devoted to Jesus Christ, although he had plans to do that, too (see *ASC*, pp. 147–48). Nevertheless, the ensemble of his thought has rightly been called Christocentric. In the final analysis, the two unwritten books on mysticism and Jesus Christ became one and the same book, for Christ is the enabler, the basis and the chief focus of Christian mysticism.

On the other hand, de Lubac himself admits that the lack of an explicitly Christological dimension, for instance, in his book *Sur les chemins de Dieu* (1956), was a genuine omission. His friend and teacher Joseph Huby had criticized the fact that the knowledge of God mediated by Christ, along with the Trinity as the specifically Christian understanding of God, are mentioned only at the conclusion. "By delaying too long among the problems of natural theology [the philosophical doctrine concerning God], one does indeed run the risk of forgetting how abstract the method is, and allowing oneself to be caught in a sort of 'religious philosophy' which usurps the place of religion itself" (*DG*, pp. 216–17).

The problem is similar in the book *Surnaturel*. There is never any doubt that Christ is the One in whom light is shed upon the riddle that man is to himself, and that only by the grace of Christ can the communion of the Triune God be recognized as the final end of man, which is also capable of practical fulfillment. The discussions in *Surnaturel*, of course, move about within an abstract framework that is logically one step prior to these truths (see the Preface to *MS*), which can lead to misunderstandings.

De Lubac's Christocentric Thinking

De Lubac's theological education began with an extra-curricular study of the article "Jesus Christ", by Léonce de Grandmaison, S.J., accompanied by a personal meeting and friendship with the author. The article was published in the *Dictionnaire d'Apologétique*, an encyclopedic reference work that presents all of theological knowledge in essays that are sometimes extremely voluminous. The article on Jesus Christ, too, fills not only a few pages, but it contains as much material as a book: in two hundred fifty columns of small print a complete *Christology* is offered, with an extensive biblical foundation, a systematic development as well as a discussion of contemporary controversies. The *Christology* and *soteriology* (doctrine concerning salvation) of the Catholic Church are presupposed by de Lubac rather than elaborated. This is entirely in keeping with his assigned duties as a fundamental theologian. With his basic apologetic concerns as his starting point, de Lubac's statements about Jesus Christ, accordingly, are situated in the field prior to dogmatic theology, for instance, when he emphasizes again and again the uniqueness of Jesus in the history of religion by using the expression *Christian novelty* or insists on the personal dimension of God's self-communication in Jesus within the framework of the question of our understanding of revelation.

Christianity has brought something absolutely new into the world. "Its concept of salvation is not merely novel in comparison with that of those religions in existence at the time of its birth. It is a unique phenomenon in the religious history of mankind" (*Cath*, p. 137).

Christian Novelty

Two mutually complementary developments in modern intellectual history led in the nineteenth century to the hey-day of the so-called "history-of-religion" school of thought.

The background for this was, on the one hand, the rapid growth in knowledge about religious phenomena [world-wide]. Added to this, on the other hand, was the denial of the revelatory character of the Christian religion in the worldview of *deism*.[1] The classical eighteenth-century author Gotthold Ephraim Lessing had already depicted Judaism, Christianity and Islam as being of equal value in his famous "Parable of the Ring" (a passage from his drama *Nathan the Wise Man*). In the so-called liberal-Protestant theology of the nineteenth century, this supported the view that all "religions" (to the extent that one accepts this term as a category encompassing Christianity as well) were in the final analysis equivalent, merely culturally different expressions of one basic human religiosity. Revelation as the self-communication of an other-worldly God within the confines of space and time is excluded a priori from the deistic worldview. On that hypothesis, even Christianity would not be the result of God's search for man, to whom he gives himself, allowing himself

---

[1] Deism, a rationalistic Enlightenment philosophy, holds that a divine being or principle (the "clockmaker God") did call the world and its physical laws into being but then left this creation to run by itself. It contradicts the Christian faith in a God who acts in history.

to be known in the one Mediator, the God-man Jesus Christ. Instead, it would be, like all other religions, only the expression of man's search for God, which by definition cannot bridge the chasm that gapes between the world and the transcendent God. Viewed in this way, the individual expressions of religion can be interpreted, indeed, as more or less successful attempts to objectify the transcendent orientation of man. The Church would have to renounce her exclusive claim to the fullness of truth and the missionary obligation that is based upon it. When liberal-Protestant theology spoke about Christianity's claim to be absolute, this meant a "relative" claim to absolute truth, inasmuch as the comparatively most advanced culture in the world developed as a result of Christianity ("cultural" Protestantism). This assessment met its definitive end with the First World War. The shared responsibility for the war and its consequences caused every feeling of cultural superiority to vanish. One still finds in the writings of many theologians the tendency to equate seemingly similar phenomena in different cultures, without taking the actual differences into account. Even today some scholars continue to maintain theories about the dependence of Jesus' title "the Son of God" on Egyptian or Greek notions, thus casually lumping the Christian belief in the Triune God with triads of Egyptian gods. In their view, Marian devotion is nothing more than a Christian variation on the Hellenistic cult of Artemis of Ephesus, and so forth.

In his historical studies, de Lubac repeatedly has to take issue with these positions.[2] He points out, often at the level

---

[2] Henri de Lubac took issue with the indiscriminate identification of the phenomena found in various religions, particularly in the essay "The Light of Christ" (1949), which was published in the collection *Theology in History*, vol. 2, *Disputed Questions and Resistance to Nazism*, trans. Anne Englund Nash (San Francisco: Ignatius Press, 1996), pp. 201–20.

of purely historical inquiry, the unprecedented and unique character of the Christian message in the history of religion. For example, de Lubac makes clear the difference between Christian faith in the Triune God and the notions of God found in Greek philosophy. It is true that Plato and Aristotle arrived at a remarkable concept of God. The Church Fathers marvel that an inkling of God should appear even in the writings of the Greek philosophers. For Aristotle, God is "living spirit", "thought about thought". But what a difference there is between this and the living, Triune God, to whose action in history both Israel and the Church testify!

> [T]hat eternal and perfect living being [the God of Aristotle] is eternally unaware of us imperfect beings; no movement of love makes him turn even a glance towards us, and therefore, in return, "only a madman would say that he loved Zeus" (Aristotle, *Ethics*, 2, 11, 1208b). But since the time of Plato and Aristotle, "a light had shone forth in our sky" (Clement of Alexandria, *Protreptikos*, 11, 114, 1) and all is new. . . . The "beatific vision" is no longer the contemplation of a spectacle but rather an intimate participation in the vision the Son has of the Father in the bosom of the Trinity. Revelation, by making us know in his Son the God of love, the personal and trinitarian God, the creating and saving God, the God "who was made man to make us God", has changed everything (*MS*, pp. 298–99).

According to de Lubac, the spiritual revolution that is initiated with the Christ-event cannot remain hidden even from a historian who methodically ignores the faith, provided that he is really ready to observe the phenomena. On the basis of the Christ-event, Christian theology and the life of the Church implicated all theological themes and concepts in a thoroughgoing process of transformation.

Of course, in examining this revolution, the ability to

make distinctions is required in a high degree, for the Incarnation of the Divine Logos did not occur in a spiritual vacuum. The Incarnation took place within a rich, complex culture with numerous intellectual currents, in the midst of different linguistic and conceptual worlds; those who unexpectedly found that they were now being ordered to witness to an unthinkable and unprecedented event could not simply break out of their cultural context. It is in no way prejudicial to the originality of Christianity if one rediscovers within it a wealth of traditions. For, as de Lubac explains, one is not original only when one coins new terminology. It depends on the subject-matter itself, which should be understood unconditionally in its distinctiveness. What is new about Jesus Christ is not primarily a new morality or an explanation of the world. What is new is Christ himself as the divine self-revelation. In his book *Paradoxes*, de Lubac summarized what he means:

> Christianity, it is said, owes this, that and the other to Judaism. It has borrowed this, that and the other from Hellenism. Or from Essenism. Everything in it is mortgaged from birth. . . .
>
> Are people naïve enough to believe, before making a detailed study, that the supernatural excludes the possession of any earthly roots and any human origin? So they open their eyes and thereby shut them to what is essential, or, to put it better, to everything: whence has Christianity borrowed Jesus Christ?
>
> However: *Omnem novitatem attulit semetipsum afferens* [He brought all novelty by bringing himself—Irenaeus of Lyons, *Adversus Haereses*, 4, 34].[3]

---

[3] *PF*, p. 215; here restoring the patristic wording, for which the English translator of *Paradoxes* had substituted 2 Cor 5:17.

Jesus Is the Christ

After the Council, de Lubac had to watch as an assertion made by Protestant exegetes gained more and more adherents among Catholic theologians as well: that the simple rabbi Jesus, who indeed distinguished himself by his extraordinary religious gift but in principle did not go beyond the parameters of what is human, gradually, over the course of the first few Christian generations, came to be understood in an exalted way as the Son of God. Proponents of this theory speak of "the Jesus of history" and "the Jesus of faith" and about a Hellenization of Christianity. This had already been maintained in the Enlightenment period (such as by Lessing), and at the time of the Modernist crisis in the early twentieth century the thesis was pondered for the first time by Catholic theologians, as well. Yet it fails for the simple reason that it is self-contradictory, as de Lubac demonstrates with the following passage taken from Hans Urs von Balthasar:

> It takes a strange mistrust of everything plausible in order to accept the notion that this figure could arise from the sheer imaginative power of some community or of some individual editor [i.e., compiler of oral traditions]. If the tranquil straightforwardness of the path that led Jesus to his demise were a subsequent fabrication of his disciples, then they must have had such a superhuman religious genius that it far surpassed that of their prototype.[4]

In countering the attenuation of Jesus as a mere myth within the framework of a mythological understanding of religion (as proposed today by Eugen Drewermann, for example), de

---

[4] Henri de Lubac, *L'Église dans la crise actuelle* (1969), p. 47, citing Hans Urs von Balthasar, *Herrlichkeit* 1:397; Eng. ed. *The Glory of the Lord*, vol. 1, trans. Erasmo Leiva-Merikakis (San Francisco: Ignatius Press, 1982).

Lubac emphasizes the event-character and the genuine histo-ricity of Jesus, of his words and deeds, of the Cross and the Resurrection.

Event, Not Myth

De Lubac speaks about the *fait du Christ* or else about *l'acte du Christ*; both expressions can probably best be translated by "Christ-event". This event comprises the whole public min-istry, the suffering and death, as well as the Resurrection and ascension and the sending of the Holy Spirit. Jesus of Naza-reth appeared on the scene claiming to be the eschatological mediator of salvation, or, as Origin incisively put it, the *auto-basileia*,[5] the Kingdom of God in person; he was handed over by the leaders of the people to the Romans, who sentenced him to death and crucified him. His disciples profess that God acknowledged Christ's Sonship by raising him from the dead, and that God thus confirms Jesus' claim and simultaneously has proved wrong those who opposed this claim. The risen Lord, by the power of the Holy Spirit, is present in the Church, his Body and his Bride, until the end of time. His proclamation of the Kingdom of God has not failed, but rather was confirmed when he rose from the dead on Easter morning, and this proclamation abides in the Church, the Body of Christ, by the power of the Holy Spirit, until the consummation of history.

In the Christ-event, the salvation history of Israel reaches its culmination. In its incomparable uniqueness and novelty, it rules over all of history, has numerous retroactive effects and brings forth all light and all spiritual fruitfulness. Together with Rousselot, de Lubac summarizes: "Christianity is based

[5] Origen, *Commentary on the Gospel of Matthew*, 14.7.

on an event, the Christ-event, the earthly life of Jesus, and Christians are those who believe today that he lives." [6]

This event is without parallel in the history of religion. Even someone who does not believe in Christ and his claim to revelation, or who because of his historical-critical perspective methodically ignores that claim, can still record the historical consequences that proceed from this event. From the very beginning, the Christian view of man exerted a compelling charm, which accounts in large measure for the success of the missionary efforts.

> Through it, man was freed, in his own eyes, from the ontological slavery with which Fate burdened him. . . . Man, every man, no matter who, had a direct link with the Creator, the Ruler of the stars themselves. . . . It was no longer a small and select company which, thanks to some secret means of escape, could break the charmed circle: it was mankind as a whole which found its night suddenly illumined and took cognisance of its royal liberty. No more circle [i.e., endlessly repeating cycle]! No more blind hazard [i.e., Fate]! . . . Hence that intense feeling of gladness and of radiant newness to be found everywhere in early Christian writings (*DAH*, p. 5).

The extraordinary explosive power of the Christ-event was demonstrated especially in the field of interpreting the previous religious tradition of Israel. De Lubac maintains that any historian can observe the extraordinary turmoil that resulted from this event. In all the history of religion, there is nothing like this process, whereby in a single stroke, because of that event, the entire religious tradition of Israel was interpreted with a boundless freedom and unheard-of self-confidence as referring to Christ. The consistency with

---

[6] Henri de Lubac, *La Révélation divine* (1968), p. 45.

which this occurred cannot be compared with any of the applications that were made within Old Testament salvation history (e.g., the interpretation of the end of the Babylonian exile as a new Exodus), nor with the allegorizing explanations[7] that were attempted within the framework of interpreting Hellenistic myths (e.g., identifying Saturn, who devoured his children, as "time", which devours everything that it brings forth). In and of itself, this observation, which the unprejudiced historian is capable of making, should caution scholars against drawing hasty parallels with seemingly comparable processes in Greek antiquity or even within the Old Testament.

Probably de Lubac's most important contribution to an understanding of Jesus Christ is his personal understanding of revelation, which continues along the lines of patristic theology. It already informs his discussions in *Exégèse médiévale*; and after the Council—relying on his preparatory studies—made this understanding the basis for the Dogmatic Constitution on Divine Revelation, *Dei Verbum*, he explained it in a detailed commentary on that document. The opening words *Dei Verbum*, "The Word of God", are programmatic and indicate the contents of the entire document in a nutshell.

Dei Verbum—Word of God

Who or what is meant by these opening words, which in the original document are printed in capital letters? *DEI VERBUM religiose audiens et fidenter proclamans* ("Hearing the WORD OF GOD with reverence and proclaiming it in faith . . ."). At first, one might be tempted to think that the subject here is the Word of Sacred Scripture. Yet the context makes it

---

[7] On the subject of allegory, see the further discussion, below, pp. 192–96.

unmistakably clear: The Word of God here refers first and foremost to the incarnate Word of God, Jesus Christ himself. About him it says in the First Letter of John: "We proclaim to you the eternal life which was with the Father and was made manifest to us—that which we have seen and heard we proclaim also to you, so that you may have fellowship with us; and our fellowship is with the Father and with his Son Jesus Christ" (1 Jn 1:2–3, as cited in *Dei Verbum* 1). With that, the contents of divine revelation, its specific character, the form in which it is handed on and its ultimate purpose are all spelled out. The content of revelation is eternal life, but that life is God himself. God has made it possible for us to experience him in Jesus Christ within the restrictions of space and time as the man Jesus of Nazareth: we have seen and heard him, the Apostle says. God, therefore, does not reveal something that is different from himself (for example, bits of information about himself), but rather reveals his very self. This life, which is God himself and which was heard and seen, is handed on when disciples bear witness to it and proclaim it. This testimony, in turn, establishes fellowship among the believers. And yet this fellowship is not the ultimate purpose of God's self-communication. It leads to fellowship with God the Father and the Son, in which revelation reaches its final goal. Thus Jesus is also God's way to men, just as he conversely takes up into himself all the ways of men to God and directs them to the Father.

In describing divine revelation as God's self-revelation and placing Christ at the center of it as the living WORD of the Father, the Second Vatican Council accentuates nuances that were implicit in the Church's previous doctrinal proclamations. The First Vatican Council also taught that divine revelation is God's communication of *himself*, which thus establishes *communicatio* and leads to *communio*, even though a more intellectual understanding of revelation prevailed in the earlier Council: revelation as the communication of truths "about" God and his salvific will. The perspective of the Second Vatican Council, which focuses more on salvation history, was no doubt prepared for by the revival of the patristic tradition, which de Lubac promoted.

The identification of the revelation-event with Jesus Christ represents another further step with respect to earlier magisterial documents. In his 1937 encyclical *Mit brennender Sorgen*, in which he rejects the ideology of National Socialism, Pope Pius XI had written that in Jesus Christ, the Son of God made man, "the fullness of divine revelation has appeared". Now *Dei Verbum* says that "[Jesus] Christ . . . is himself both the mediator and the sum total of Revelation" (*Dei Verbum* no. 2).

Christ: The Source of Revelation

With that, the long-debated question as to the "sources of revelation" is also settled. In the course of controversies with Protestant theology and the debate concerning Scripture and Tradition, scholars discussed whether Scripture and Tradition were two sources of revelation, since the Council of Trent allegedly spoke about two sources (*fontes*), leading to the "Two-Source Theory". Yet even Trent knew of only one source of Tradition, since in reality it spoke about *fons* (source) in the singular. Cardinal Frings of Cologne made the decisive breakthrough at the Council by distinguishing between *fons essendi* (source of being) and *fontes inveniendi* (literally: sources of discovery, i.e., of transmission). Christ, because he is the WORD OF GOD, is the one true source of revelation. Sacred Scripture and Tradition are modes in which revelation is handed on and thus are not "sources" in the same sense as Christ is, but rather sources in the sense of means of transmitting revelation (*EVII*, pp. 49–50; *ATS*, p. 18).

Christianity Is Not a "Religion of the Book"

Without diminishing the importance of Sacred Scripture as an obligatory witness to revelation, what all this means for the self-understanding of Christianity is that—unlike Islam, for instance—Christianity is not a "religion of the book", as de Lubac never tired of emphasizing. The Church's faith is concerned first and foremost with a personal relationship to Jesus Christ, who in the Holy Spirit reestablishes fellowship among us and with the Father. In this connection, de Lubac recalled an intervention of the Archbishop of Ougadougou, Upper Volta, Paul Zoungrana, who spoke in the name of sixty-seven African bishops at the Council as follows:

> Fundamentally, Christ himself is the Revelation that he brings. . . . The truths that we are to believe and the duties that we are to perform should be seen above all as they are related to a living person. Tell the world that divine revelation is Christ. The beautiful face of Christ must shine more clearly in the Church. In that way you will renew the miraculous signs of love and fidelity that were resplendent in the early Church (cited in *EVII*, p. 51).

Christ: The New Testament in Person

In Christ, the incarnate WORD of God, the prototype of the oneness of God's Word is given in a human word, whereby God's self-communication in Jesus Christ is not restricted to his words but, rather, encompasses his words and deeds, in fact the entire Christ-event. "Jesus Christ is the Gospel in person"; he is "the New Testament in person"; de Lubac cites, among other medieval theologians who said this, Amalarius of Metz (*Liber officialis* II, 20). Since it is not primarily a matter of a reference to a book but, rather, of a relationship to a Person, we can speak—alluding to a provocative book title—about a "Christianity without the New Testament", provided that we understand by this the collection of writings that resulted in the second half of the first century from the process of committing Christian witness to writing. The first martyrs of the Church died for their faith in Jesus Christ, without ever having held a New Testament in their hands. If, however, we understand the New Testament as something personal from the very beginning, then the slogan just mentioned is self-contradictory. There is no Christianity without Christ. Now, when the eyewitnesses of Jesus, who heard his preaching with their own ears, were proclaiming the Gospel by the power of the Holy Spirit, their proclamation had no other contents than the salvation-event in Christ Jesus, his words, his deeds, but especially his suffering, his death on the Cross and his victorious Resurrection. The witness concerning the one WORD of God is handed on in the human words of those who had encountered him and who, enlightened by the Holy Spirit, recognized him as the definitive bearer of salvation, as the One who reveals the Father. That is why Paul can say that his proclamation of Christ to the Thessalonians, too (as also to the other congregations) is God's word in human words. "And we also thank God constantly for this, that when you received the word of God which you heard from us, you accepted it not as the word of men but as what it really is, the word of God, which is at work in you believers" (1 Thess 2:13). That is also why, after the reading during the Liturgy of the Word, whether it is taken from the Old or the New Testament, we can rightly say, "The Word of the Lord", for the human words of Scripture ultimately give witness—by way of anticipation in the Old Testament, immediately in the New—to the one WORD of God, which is the incarnate Son of the Father.

Fulfillment of the Old Testament

Jesus Christ is the definitive WORD of the Father; the *Logos* is the Son (Jn 1:16, 18), but it is not his first word. For, as the Letter to the Hebrews says, "In many and various ways God spoke of old to our fathers by the prophets", even before God spoke to us in these last days through his Son (Heb 1:1–2). Through his self-communication in Jesus Christ, it becomes clear that the Sacred Scriptures of Israel, too, can be and are God's fully valid Word. For God is no "lonely", self-enclosed God; rather, he fulfills his divine nature in the inner relatedness of Father, Son and Spirit. In and of himself, God is communication, exchange; in him there is the distinction between thinking and what is thought, between speaking and word, between love and the beloved. Consequently, he can also communicate himself to the creature without losing his divinity. Another reason that this communication is free is because God does not need it for the sake of his own perfection (see *Cath*, pp. 329ff.).

Verbum Abbreviatum[8]—The Abridged Word

The idea that the many words of God were summarized in the one WORD, which is the Son of God, was taken up in the Middle Ages especially by theologians from the Cistercian Order, who were fond of preaching on this subject in Advent

[8] A chapter with the same title in one of the later volumes of *Medieval Exegesis* has not yet been translated into English. See chap. 3.3 of de Lubac's *Scripture in Tradition*.

and on Christmas. The biblical points of departure were the Prologue to John's Gospel (Jn 1:1–18), the beginning of the Letter to the Hebrews (Heb 1:1–2), as well as a verse from the Letter to the Romans, which in turn cites an expression from the Book of the Prophet Isaiah. In the Vulgate,[9] the verse reads:"*Verbum (ab)breviatum faciet Dominus super terram*— A short word shall the Lord make upon the earth" (Rom 9:28 [Douay-Rheims], citing Is 10:23 ["an abridgment in the midst of all the land"]. Many modern Bible translations make it difficult to discern either the allusion or the etymology.) In Jesus, the Father's Word made flesh, the word of the prophet has been fulfilled: Jesus is personally the abridged, abbreviated Word that sums up all the many words. Guerric (1070 or 1081–1157), the Abbot of Igny, a student of Saint Bernard of Clairvaux,[10] preaches as follows about the Christmas Gospel:

> If we piously and attentively listen to this Word, which the Lord has brought forth today and shown to us, how much we can learn from him, and how easily! For it is, in a sense, an abbreviated word, yet shortened in such a way that it sums up within it every word that serves the purpose of salvation. For "it is a word that summarizes and shortens in righteousness" [Is 10:28, Vulgate, which numbers the verses differently]. . . . Yet is it not astonishing that the Word of God should have abbreviated all his words to us when It willed to be abbreviated itself and made insignificant, so to speak, that it somehow contracted its immeasurable greatness and entered the confines of a mother's womb, and that he who holds the world in his hands allowed himself to be laid in a crib?[11]

---

[9] The *Vulgata* means, literally, "the generally circulated [version]". It designates the Latin translation of the Bible prepared by St. Jerome (347–419), which was the official version of the Catholic Church.

[10] Concerning St. Bernard, see below, pp. 216–17, n. 3.

[11] *In nativitate Domini*, sermo 5.3.

The Church: Sacrament and Mother

Today the doctrine about the Church (*ecclesiology*) is a standard component of dogmatic theology. This was not always the case. Until well into the Middle Ages, the Church did not explicitly make herself a theological theme. The Church was believed, along with other doctrines, as a work of the Holy Spirit; more precisely, Christians believed *in her*, from her the faith was received, she guaranteed the continuity of the transmission and the truth of scriptural interpretation. She was, so to speak, the atmosphere in which the Christian breathed and faith flourished. Many causes led to the emergence of the theme the Church herself on the horizon of explicit theological reflection: the reform movements in Church history, but especially divisions in the Church raised the question of the true Church and the conditions for membership. After the first beginnings in the late medieval period, in connection with the controversies about the relationship between a council and the Pope, finally, in the nineteenth century—with the so-called Tübingen and Roman Schools playing a decisive role—systematic treatises were composed about the Church, her nature, her founding, her specific constitution and other similar questions.

The Church's Magisterium did not formulate the Church's understanding of herself in a comprehensive way until the Second Vatican Council and the Dogmatic Constitution on the Church, *Lumen gentium*.

Henri de Lubac contributed significant insights to this still recent treatise on the Church as well.

His reflections on the Church are accompanied by the clear awareness that this concern with herself can be dangerous to the Church also, for two reasons. First, the concern with herself can cripple her by leading to "navel-gazing". De Lubac observes, "It would seem as if there were in this reflexive activity a danger such as that which threatens the man who wants to be a spectator at his own prayer. For if you turn back in contemplation of yourself instead of contemplating the object of your faith and invoking that of your hope, the recoil and self-regarding involved seem likely to put a sort of filter between your spiritual vision and the reality that is the object of the faith and hope alike" (*SpCh*, p. 20). The other danger is that the Church might mistake herself for the light that she is supposed to reflect. *Lumen gentium*, meaning "Light of the Nations", the opening words of the Dogmatic Constitution on the Church, which state its theme, do not refer to the Church, however, but to Christ. Repeatedly, de Lubac points out the Christocentric nature of the Council, noting that this was illustrated by the gesture of Pope Paul VI,[1] who in January of 1964 became the first Pope in several hundred years to travel abroad when he left the Vatican on a pilgrimage to the Holy Land.

> Paul VI went, in the name of the whole Church, to prostrate himself before the Holy Sepulcher, to show that all Christians are the faithful followers of Christ. He went to give witness that the Church is nothing if she is not the handmaid of Christ, if she does not reflect his Light, if she does not transmit

[1] After the death of Pope John XXIII on June 3, 1963, the Archbishop of Milan, Giovanni B. Cardinal Montini, was elected his successor on June 21, and he took the name Paul VI (1897–1978).

his Life. He wanted to be, like Pope Honorius III in the famous mosaic of St. Paul's-Outside-the-Walls, literally bowed down to the earth and of minuscule dimensions before an enormous, upright Christ in majesty (*ATS*, pp. 9–10).

The Church has been called into question, however. Therefore she herself must clearly understand her own nature, even though being concerned with herself involves certain risks.

Credo Ecclesiam

But has the Church not been mentioned expressly in the profession of faith since the earliest times? Indeed, both the great Niceno-Constantinopolitan Creed[2] and the Apostles' Creed, which is used particularly in the devotions of the Western Church, mention the Church immediately in connection with the belief in the Holy Spirit. In his early lectures on the Church and later again in great detail in his book *La Foi chrétienne: Essai sur la structure du Symbole des Apôtres* (1970),[3] de Lubac explains the particular mode of Christian faith with reference to the Church. The Latin verb *credo* (presumably derived from *cor do* = "I give my heart") can be understood in three ways: (1) *Credo Deum esse* = "I believe that God exists"; (2) *Credo Deo* = "I believe God", "I entrust myself to him"; a third way is the specifically Christian mode that comes from biblical usage: (3) *Credo in Deum* = "I believe *in* God", "I believe *unto* God." Behind this last formula is the Hebrew idea of faith as the state of being anchored in God, of

---

[2] Named after the first two Ecumenical Councils, held in Nicaea (325) and Constantinople (381), which professed this great Creed as the expression of the Christian faith.

[3] *The Christian Faith: An Essay on the Structure of the Apostles' Creed*, trans. Richard Arnandez (San Francisco: Ignatius Press, 1986).

being moored securely in God, as it then says in the Gospel of John: "Let not your hearts be troubled; believe in God, believe also in me" (Jn 14:1). To believe in God means to acknowledge him, to do him homage, to worship him, to commend oneself and one's entire life to him, to believe unto him [as one's destination] in the unity of faith, hope and love. In remaining true to this biblical usage, the early Christians did not hesitate to offend the linguistic sensibilities of Greek and then Latin speakers by translating the expression literally as *pisteuein eis* (Greek) and *credere in* (Latin). Yet this too belongs to the novelty of the Christian message: thought and language are broadened and enriched with new possibilities for expression.

This phrase, *credere in*, refers exclusively to the Divine Persons. Only in God can one believe in this way. When we speak in the third part of the Creed about believing "in" the Church as well, we should note that in the Latin version there is no preposition "in": *Credo ecclesiam*. De Lubac recalls that in the beginning, when the Church was mentioned, it was probably designated as the sole place in which faith in the Triune God can be professed, somewhat along these lines: I believe in God, the Father, the Son and the Holy Spirit, in the assembly of his Church. Christians "believe the Church" in the same way that they testify to their faith that heaven and earth are created by God the Father Almighty, that there is an Incarnation, a death, a Resurrection and an ascension of Jesus Christ. By mentioning the Church in the Creed, the Christian acknowledges the Church as a work of the Holy Spirit, and he affirms that she transmits to him the faith in which he finds salvation, the communion of saints, the forgiveness of sins and the resurrection to everlasting life.

A preconciliar magisterial document on the Church, written by Pope Pius XII in the year 1943, bore the richly significant title *Mystici corporis* and was centered on the Pauline image of the Church as the Body of Christ (1 Cor 10:16). The Holy Spirit is described as the Soul of this Body.

In the year 1939, just before the promulgation of that encyclical, de Lubac had completed his work *Corpus mysticum*. The war delayed its publication.

Corpus Mysticum—The Mystical Body

In this study, de Lubac begins with an historical investigation of the association of the terms *"mysticum"* and *"corpus Christi"* and arrives at the underlying relationship between Eucharist and Church.

Ever since the bull *Unam Sanctam* of Pope Boniface VIII (1302), the expression *Corpus mysticum* has seemed to be the perennially valid description of the Church. De Lubac demonstrates, however, that the formula "mystical body" (in its Greek form, *soma mysticon*) is found for the first time in the work of the theologian Hesychius of Jerusalem (who died in the mid-fifth century) and made its way into the works of ninth-century Western theologians via Latin translations. Now, in all of these authors, *Corpus mysticum* does not mean the Church but, rather, the Eucharistic Body of our Lord (as distinguished from the historical and glorified Body of Christ). Conversely, in the writings of Augustine, the expression *Corpus Christi verum* (the true Body of Christ) refers to the Church. In chapter 25 of book 21 of *The City of God*, in which Augustine speaks about membership in the Church as a necessary prerequisite for the proper reception of the sacraments, he also discusses the ringleaders of the heretical teachers, who were once baptized in the Catholic Church and received the sacraments in the "true Body of Christ", which is the Church, but to no avail (*De Civitate Dei*, XXI, 25, 3).

Not until the eleventh century is a fundamental change in linguistic usage introduced. The occasion for this is the symbolic interpretation of the Eucharist by the theologian Berengar of Tours (c. 1005–1088).

Only Symbolic?

Berengar proposes the view that the consecrated elements of bread and wine represent the Body and Blood of Christ, but are not essentially changed. Berengar was excommunicated, but later on submitted to the Church's Magisterium and assented to the required formulas of faith. From the controversy with him there resulted a stronger emphasis on the Real Presence, that is, the true presence of Christ in the Eucharist. And so gradually the adjectives changed: the Eucharistic Body became the *Corpus Christi verum*, whereas the Church became the *Corpus Christi mysticum* (the earliest attestation is found in Magister Simon in his *Tractatus de sacramentis*, around 1170.[4] De Lubac shows how the Church now gradually disappears from view also as a mystery of faith because— unlike in the writings of the Church Fathers—"mystic" is increasingly understood in the sense of "only spiritual", as opposed to real, tangible and visible. The connection between Eucharist and Church, which should be recovered with reference to 1 Corinthians 10:16, is a mutually constitutive relationship: Church and Eucharist are founded upon each other. De Lubac coined an expression for this that was often repeated at the Council: "The Church produces the Eucharist, and the Eucharist produces the Church." With every celebration of the Eucharist, the Church receives her being anew as the Body of Christ, so that in the Holy Spirit

---

[4] See Henri de Lubac, *Corpus mysticum: L'Eucharistie et l'Église au Moyen Âge* (Paris: Aubier-Montaigne, 1949), p. 130.

she can be the Real Presence of Christ in the world. To put it another way, in the words of Augustine, who exclaims to the faithful in the sermon: "If you are the Body of Christ, then the sacrament that you yourselves are is placed upon the Lord's table; you receive the sacrament that you yourselves are. You respond to what you receive with 'Amen' and you ratify it by responding to it. You hear the words, 'The Body of Christ', and you answer 'Amen'. Be therefore a member of Christ, so that your Amen may be genuine" (*Sermo* 272).

De Lubac treats further ecclesiological themes in a series of conferences that he gave to priests in the years immediately after the Second World War, which were published as the book *The Splendor of the Church*. We will mention only a few selected themes from it.

The Church—Paradox and Mystery

The Church is an object of the faith. This is what is meant by the expression "the Church is a Mystery". Furthermore, this expresses the fact that the Church, like her Lord, unites divine and human elements.

The Church, which was already foreseen in the plan of creation, constituted as the covenant people of Israel in the Exodus from Egypt and gathered together as a renewed covenant people by Jesus Christ, is ultimately the work of the Holy and Sanctifying Spirit, who permeates the Body of Christ as its living soul. The Church bears witness to the Gospel; by the power of the Holy Spirit she brings forth Sacred Scripture as a testimonial to revelation, and in her is accomplished the entire work of salvation. She is the "continuation of Christ", the extension of Christ's Incarnation through history. "The mystery of the Church is all Mystery in miniature; it is our own mystery par excellence. It lays hold on the whole of us. It surrounds us on all sides, for it is in his Church that God looks upon us and loves us, in her that he desires us and we encounter him, and in her that we cleave to him and are made blessed by him" (*SpCh*, pp. 45–46).

At the same time, the Church is also fully human. She cannot say, as her Lord does, "Which of you convicts me of sin?" (Jn 8:46). The mediocrity and sinfulness of Christians, the fragility of the vessels to which God has entrusted his salvation in Jesus Christ, is distressing. Here an even greater paradox becomes apparent than the mystery of the Son of God made man. "If a purification and transformation of vision is necessary to look on Christ without being scandalized, how much more is it necessary when we are looking at the Church! Here it will be even more essential—if we are to reach some understanding of her—to 'cast far from us the darkness of earthly reasoning and the mists of the wisdom of this world'" (*SpCh*, p. 50, citing St. Leo the Great, *Sermo* 7).

In any case, the inadequacy of the Church is not the sole reason why she may be rejected. Like her Lord, she must be prepared to be understood quite well precisely when she proclaims the Word of God most faithfully and to be rejected for that very reason. "She is the permanent witness of Christ and the messenger of the living God; his urgent and importunate presence among us. Let us within the Church, who speak of ourselves as being 'of the Church', manage to grasp the fact as sharply as it is sensed by those who are afraid of her and those who run away from her" (*SpCh*, p. 50).

The Common Priesthood and the Special [Ministerial] Priesthood

Did Christ give a share of his high-priestly ministry to his Church only as a whole, or did he institute within her a special priesthood, which he equipped with his full authority and ordered to carry out a special ministry? Down to the present day, this question points up one of the chief differences between the Catholic Church and the churches of the Reformation. Luther, citing especially 1 Peter 2:5–9 ("But you are a chosen race, a royal priesthood"), argued against a sacramental priesthood instituted by Jesus Christ for and in his Church. For Luther and the other Reformers, the ministry of proclaiming the Word and administering the sacraments is something instituted by the Church and is thus not of divine but of merely human right—something that is left up to the Church to modify and adapt to changing situations. At the Council of Trent (1545–1563) the Catholic Church, in reaction to Luther, reaffirmed her faith that the Lord himself gave to the Church the ministerial priesthood, which developed into the three orders: bishop, presbyter,[5] and deacon, whereby it is the responsibility of the bishop and the presbyter to offer the Eucharistic Sacrifice.

This might give the impression that the Catholic Church knows only of the ministerial priesthood, whereas the Evangelical [Lutheran] church, apparently in greater conformity to the biblical testimony, upholds the common priesthood of all believers.

In one section of the chapter from *The Splendor of the Church* entitled "The Heart of the Church" (pp. 133–44), de Lubac objects to this false alternative. Based on the anthology of sources compiled by his Jesuit confrère Paul Dabin, who

[5] The English word *priest* (Greek *presbyteros*; Old French *prestre*) is a ministerial title that in Greek literally means "advanced in age (or rank)". In the New Testament, it is a name for officials who exercised the ministry of leadership together with the bishops [*episkopoi*] as successors to the Apostles. Although at first the office was not clearly distinguished from the episcopal ministry, by the second century, *presbyteros* was the title for those who had received the second degree of Holy Orders.

researched the testimonies of the Church's understanding of the common priesthood of all believers down through the centuries and presented them with commentary in a voluminous book, de Lubac recalls that during the patristic and the Scholastic periods, no opposition whatsoever was seen between the common priesthood and the special or ministerial priesthood.

Pope Leo the Great, for instance, extolled the dignity of the common priesthood on the occasion of his consecration:

> Although the universal Church of God is constituted of distinct orders of members, still, in spite of the many parts of its holy body, the Church subsists as an integral whole, just as the Apostle says: "We are all one in Christ" (see Gal 3:28), nor is anyone separated from the office of another in such a way that a lower group has no connection with the head. In the unity of faith and baptism, our community is then undivided. There is a common dignity. . . . For all regenerated in Christ are made kings by the sign of the cross; they are consecrated priests by the oil of the Holy Spirit.[6]

More than a hundred years earlier, Augustine had expressed himself in a very similar way. In a sermon on the anniversary of his episcopal consecration, he emphasized that the ministry conferred upon him does not incapacitate or disenfranchise the members of the Church, but rather that he is commissioned to the service of the Church. "Whereas [this office] frightens me in what I am for you, it consoles me in what I am with you. *Indeed, for you I am a bishop, with you I am a Christian*. The former designates the ministry that I have received, the latter—the grace; the one is a token of danger, the other of salvation" (*Sermo* 340).

The common priesthood of all the faithful and the special

---

[6] *Sermo* 4.1, cited here from the Liturgy of the Hours, Office of Readings, November 10.

sacramental ministry in the Church, therefore, are not mutually exclusive but rather ordered to one another. The special priestly ministry of the Church is not the conferral of privileges, but rather a service to the communion of the faithful, inasmuch as the man who is appointed to the spiritual ministry represents Christ, the Head of his Church, through a special participation in his prophetic, priestly and royal office, in proclaiming the Word, in sanctifying the Church through the administration of the sacraments and in governing the Church.

After the Council, de Lubac took issue on various occasions with the attempts, even by Catholic theologians, to adopt the thesis of the liberal-Protestant history of dogma, according to which the theology of the priesthood drifted from its biblical origins over the course of the fourth century and fell back upon a Jewish or even pagan understanding of sacrificial priesthood. By citing the New Testament sources and the writings of Ignatius of Antioch, Irenaeus of Lyons and many other Apostolic Fathers, he proves the essential continuity within all the external changes (see p. 96 above).

This subject is also connected with the question of the restriction of the ordained priesthood to persons of the male sex. This becomes comprehensible only when one takes into consideration the fact that divine revelation is inscribed in created reality, in this case, in the complementary of the sexes, which is given as part of creation. De Lubac makes important points about this subject as well.

The Maternity of the Church and Spiritual Fatherhood

One of the more significant accomplishments of twentieth-century ecclesiology is the rediscovery of Mary as the "Model of the Church". De Lubac played a decisive part in this rediscovery, although he refers to other thinkers who pioneered along these lines.

Pierre Teilhard de Chardin and the poet Paul Claudel,[7] in particular, gave contemporary theologians fresh insights into the intimate connection between the figure of Mary and the Church, thus bringing Marian devotion back from the periphery of the faith and restoring it to its rightful place.

"The Holy Virgin Mary, so far as I am concerned, is the Church. I have never found any reason to distinguish between them", says Claudel, in his blunt way, whereby he actually meant, as de Lubac explains, that in his mind the two realities are indissolubly united. This insight of Claudel is very closely bound up with his conversion experience. At Vespers in Notre Dame Cathedral on Christmas Eve in 1886—a service to which he had gone out of boredom—he was overwhelmed by the impact of the Catholic faith in its entirety during the singing of the Magnificat, Mary's song of praise, and he realized how everything that is said about Mary is true of the Church, and that conversely the Church sees in Mary her perfect prototype (see *CPM*, p. 63).

Teilhard expressed this same insight in the poem "Hymn to the Eternal Feminine".[8] In parallel with his cosmic Christology, Teilhard sketches here a cosmic Mariology, which sees the "eternal feminine", the created principle of bodily and spiritual receptivity, culminating in Mary. "Do you understand now the mystery of your trembling when I draw

[7] Paul Claudel (1868–1955) was a French diplomat and poet who rediscovered, among other things, the spiritual interpretation of Scripture.

[8] Pierre Teilhard de Chardin, "Hymn to the Eternal Feminine", written in 1917, was published by de Lubac in 1965 with a commentary: English ed., *The Eternal Feminine: A Study on the Poem by Teilhard de Chardin . . .*, trans. René Hague (New York: Harper & Row, 1971).

near? . . . I am the Church, the Bride of Jesus. I am the Virgin Mary, the Mother of all mankind."

In Mary, the essence of the Church is made concrete because she makes visible the Catholic principle of the importance of man's cooperation in salvation. The Church as a whole and every individual Christian is commissioned and enabled to cooperate [with the Savior], and Mary in fact cooperated in exemplary fashion, inasmuch as God's Son was unwilling to become man without her *fiat*, her faithful consent. Thus de Lubac can agree with Karl Barth's diagnosis:

> The "Mother of God" of Roman Catholic dogma about Mary is . . . quite simply, the principle, prototype and summing-up of the *human creature* cooperating (*ministerialiter*) [as a servant] in its own salvation by making use of prevenient grace; as such, she is also the principle, prototype and summing-up of the *Church*. . . . Thus, the Church in which there is a cult of Mary *must* be itself understood as at the [First] Vatican Council; is of necessity that Church of man who, by virtue of grace, cooperates with grace.[9]

Whereas Karl Barth decisively rejects this way of viewing the Church on the basis of his Calvinist position, de Lubac regards it as a characteristic expression of the Christian understanding of God and man: "Catholic faith regarding our Lady sums up symbolically, in [her] special case, the doctrine of human cooperation in the Redemption and thus provides the synthesis, or matrix concept, as it were, of the dogma of the Church" (*SpCh*, p. 316).

As Mother, the Church gives birth to her children in baptism, and, conversely, every Christian is called to receive Christ into his heart and to allow him to take shape in his life

[9] Karl Barth, *Kirchliche Dogmatik*, vol. 1, part 2 (1938), pp. 157 and 160; cited in *SpCh*, p. 316.

(cf. the important theme of "the birth of God in the soul" that runs through all of Christian spirituality).

A counterpart to the theme of the Church's maternity is the theme of "spiritual fatherhood" and the male priest-hood.[10] Jesus represents God the Father, and inasmuch as the Apostles and their successors, by the power of the Holy Spirit, represent Jesus Christ, the Lord of the Church, the bishop too is called "father" by the Apostle Paul (1 Cor 4:15) and other early Christian writers. The fatherhood of bishops is a participation in the Fatherhood of God in Christ. Through the proclamation of the Gospel, through governing the Church and through the sanctifying sacramental ministry, they make present Christ, the One Sent by the Father, within the communion of the Church. This has nothing whatsoever to do with patriarchal rigidity or class divisions within the Church. Rather, it takes the created difference between the sexes seriously as a medium for divine revelation. The theol-ogy of the sexes is of the greatest importance for the Catholic understanding of the Church and of the entire drama of salvation involving God and man; in the writings of de Lubac this theology is sketched rather than fully developed. Still, it is based not upon a contrast between the supposedly typical female and male characteristics, but rather upon the relation of mutuality between man and woman, which is most pro-foundly sanctified in the sacrament of marriage as a real symbol of God's love for mankind. God's self-communication is inscribed within this mutual relationship when Christ, as the Father's representative, makes himself known as the Bridegroom of the Church, his Bride.

---

[10] Henri de Lubac, *Quellen kirchlicher Einheit* [Sources of Church unity] (1974), pp. 156–71.

The Fourfold Sense of Scripture

The *Catechism of the Catholic Church* (1993) recommends applying the doctrine of the "fourfold interpretation of Scripture" (par. 115–20) in order to interpret the biblical writings comprehensively. Thus, in her Profession of Faith, the Church has again taken cognizance of another theme that Henri de Lubac dealt with extensively. In a series of essays, but most especially in his book about Origen and in the four later volumes that built upon that foundation, *Exégèse médiévale* (*Medieval Exegesis*), which bear the subtitle *Les Quatre Sens de l'Écriture* (The Four Senses of Scripture), de Lubac worked out the meaning of this doctrine in its full significance, snatched it from oblivion and brought its relevant teachings into the contemporary discussion of Scripture.

A Mnemonic Verse

In order to impress this doctrine upon the memory, a distich, a couplet of rhythmic verse, was composed in the Middle Ages:

> *Littera gesta docet; quid credas allegoria;*
> *Moralis quid agas; quo tendas anagogia.*

> The letter teaches deeds and events;
> allegory, what you should believe;

the moral sense, what you should do;
and the anagogical sense, to what you
should direct your course.

Thus Sacred Scripture has four dimensions of meaning: the *literal* sense (which corresponds to history), the *allegorical* sense (which is related to faith), the *moral* sense (which regards conduct, for which love is the highest norm) and finally the *anagogical* sense (which arouses and strengthens hope).

Even at first glance, it is evident that this doctrine is not an arbitrary list of unconnected ways of looking at Scripture; rather, we can discern within it a structure that encompasses the entire Christian life in faith, love and hope.

Let us examine each sense.

The letter teaches deeds and events. This means that the Sacred Scripture of the Old and New Testaments is to be understood first of all as testimony to a historical revelation of God in his people Israel, and then in Jesus Christ as the goal and climax of that revelation. Sacred Scripture itself is not revelation, but rather a *witness* to revelation, inasmuch as the human authors, inspired by the Holy Spirit, testified in human words to events in which God himself manifested himself: God's Word in men's words. The traditional interpretation of Scripture assigns the literal sense to this first level. The development of modern exegetical science calls for a few further considerations with respect to this first level. Not every biblical text bears witness to a historical event. Today we can distinguish among different literary genres or forms, which any serious interpretation must take into account. It is nevertheless of decisive importance that Christian faith is not based on perennially valid philosophical statements or on human insights disguised as myths and fairy tales, but rather on the revelation of God in history.

Allegory, what you should believe. In a second step, which theological tradition designates as *allegoria*, we look at the theological significance of the historical event. De Lubac deserves credit for reestablishing the Christian meaning of the term *allegory*, which has so often been misunderstood. By allegory, the Church's entire Tradition understands the theological approach to Scripture, which is based on the historical foundation and explores the historical testimony so as to find therein the proclamation of God's self-communication. "Allegory builds up faith", said Gregory the Great, thus coining a classical axiom. But, with that, the Christian has not yet reached the goal of his encounter with Scripture.

The moral sense, what you should do. Scripture as a whole, and thus each passage as well, contains instruction on how to live. Scripture is aimed at the transformation of the Christian into a loving person. Even the Apostle Paul said that faith is realized in love.

The doctrine of the fourfold meaning of Scripture has eschatology as its ultimate objective.

The anagogical sense, to what you should direct your course. Anagogy (Greek *ana*, "upward", and *agein*, "to lead") is a neologism designating the final dimension into which biblical testimony extends. The Word of God to which Scripture testifies not only builds up faith and kindles the love of the Christian, but also directs his eyes in faith toward the good things that have been promised and are to be hoped for.

The Fourfold Jerusalem

A suitable illustration is the example "Jerusalem". By its very breadth, as de Lubac says, it encompasses in a way all other possible examples. The city of Jerusalem can be understood successively in a fourfold sense: Jerusalem as a historical city is the scene of Jesus' Passion and thus the site of salvation history. In the allegorical sense, Jerusalem can be seen as a symbol for the City of God (*Civitas Dei*) that has been renewed in Christ. In the moral sense, it depicts the Christian soul, into which the Lord wishes to make his entrance as he did during his earthly life into historical Jerusalem. And finally, the Book of Revelation is already familiar with the image of the heavenly Jerusalem as the city of perfection (anagogical sense).

The doctrine of the fourfold interpretation of Scripture should not be understood as though all four dimensions or senses could be demonstrated in every word or passage of Scripture. The decisive thing is the fundamental insight that there is a dynamic leading from history to faith, which is realized in love and borne up by hope. Over the course of the late Middle Ages, the doctrine of the fourfold sense of Scripture hardened into a mere formality. Luther became acquainted with it in a form that was already distorted and later rejected it; nevertheless, he remained faithful to many of its principles in his own practice of interpreting Scripture.

Not Only a Medieval Teaching

De Lubac's first important contribution was to have shown that this largely forgotten, in many ways distorted, and finally controverted, theory was not a doctrine unique to the Middle Ages; rather, it goes back to the very beginnings of the Christian faith—indeed, it is ultimately rooted in the New Testament and in its manner of referring to the Old Testament. The central role in this clarification is played by the second element in the mnemonic verse: Allegory teaches what you should believe. Hardly any other theological concept is so overlaid with misunderstandings and ambiguities. In art history, we think of "personifications" (e.g., "Allegory of Springtime"), and in contemporary Scripture scholarship, allegory most often refers to a particular sort of figure of speech: whereas an image or metaphor ordinarily places emphasis on a single point of comparison, in an allegory all the details are significant. Even in antiquity—and here we come to the most egregious misunderstanding—many who interpreted Scripture allegorically were accused of reducing the Bible to the level of pagan myths by this method. It was supposed that, like the interpreters of Greek mythology, they managed to do away with offensive passages by superimposing their own readings, thus denying the historical basis for Sacred Scripture.

Etymologically, literally, the Greek word means "saying something else". As a technical theological term, it was introduced almost simultaneously in the mid-first century by Philo of Alexandria and by the Apostle Paul in his Letter to the Galatians (4:24). In this passage, Paul interprets the two wives of Abraham as representing the two Testaments, because these things are to be understood allegorically (*hatiná estin allegoroúmena*). Allegorical interpretation is a Christological interpretation made possible by the Holy Spirit.

Unity of Scripture

This broaches the subject of the "unity of Scripture",[1] the "connection between the Old and the New Testament", which de Lubac increasingly recognized as being central for the history of scriptural exegesis and which also is the source of the doctrine of the fourfold sense of Scripture. The Old

[1] On this subject, see Rudolf Voderholzer, *Die Einheit der Schrift und ihr geistiger Sinn* [The unity of Scripture and its spiritual sense] (1996), pp. 177–234.

and New Testaments are not just externally linked, but are intimately interrelated. The middle term that joins them is Christ. The Scripture of the Old Covenant points ultimately to him, the writings of the New Testament testify to him using the characteristic expressions of the Old Covenant, and following his initiative, all the texts of the Old Covenant—even those that do not expressly contain Messianic prophecies—are interpreted with reference to Christ and the Church. Augustine expressed the principle of the unity of Old Testament and the New Testament in this way: "The New lies hidden in the Old; the Old is plainly evident in the New" (Novum in Vetere latet, Vetus in Novo patet).[2] All the major themes of the Christian faith are closely interwoven with the salvation history of the Old Covenant, so that without the Old Testament it is impossible to speak about baptism, the Eucharist, the Church, etc.

Allegory and the Spiritual Sense

Connected with the concept of allegory, which to begin with was not the only and not even the most prominent term used, are other pairs of concepts, such as letter and spirit, shadow and reality, prefiguration and fulfillment, type and antitype. In looking to Christ, the Christian receives the fullness of light, and the veil falls away from the Law, so that he can recognize its deeper meaning. In light of the Christ-event, the redemptive facts of the Old Covenant prove to be prefigurations and shadows, which find their fulfillment in the New Testament, in Christ and his Church. In the different personages of Old Testament salvation history, the Church recognizes prefigurations (types) of Christ (e.g., Adam, Jonah, David), just as

[2] St. Augustine, *Quaestiones in Heptateuchum* 2, 73; cited also in *Dei Verbum* no. 16.

Mary's cooperation in Redemption is mysteriously depicted in advance in the female figures God sent to the rescue. In the New Testament, the Psalms especially are interpreted with reference to Christ, understood as "the prayer of Christ himself" (Ps 22: "My God, my God, why hast thou forsaken me?"), as "a prayer to Christ" (Ps 31:5: "Thou has redeemed me, O Lord. . ."), or, finally, as a "prophecy about Jesus" (Ps 118:22: "The stone which the builders rejected has become the cornerstone").

A crucial point is that this Christological meaning of Old Testament Scripture cannot be discovered by merely rational inspection. Of course, the preaching of the prophets also depicts quite well the promise of a future savior; furthermore, Yahweh's historical action in his Word and in his Spirit portrays him as an autonomous, living, threefold God who intends to communicate himself.

But only with the actual incarnation of the Divine Logos, in light of the death and Resurrection of Jesus and in the power of the Holy Spirit, is the entire Old Testament transformed into a witness to Christ; then the Church, with an incomparable freedom, can apply the Scriptures of Israel to Christ with a variety of methods no longer limited to allegory, typology, midrash, and so forth. Hence theologians have spoken and continue to speak first of all, and most precisely, about a "spiritual sense" of Scripture.

The basic movement, then, at the origin of the doctrine of the fourfold sense of Scripture, is the movement from the letter of the Old Testament toward its spirit, namely, its reference to Christ.

Although at first allegorical interpretation was an interpretation of only the Old Testament (that is all that there was to begin with), later on it became possible to speak of an allegorical interpretation of the New Testament also. Thereby the

New Testament is not demoted or placed on a par with the Old; rather, as de Lubac demonstrates, this takes into account, in faith, the fact that New Testament Scripture, too, is not simply and immediately God's Word but is a testimony in human words to the Word of God, inasmuch as the one WORD, which is the Son, represents the meaningful center of the entire New Testament witness.

Origen as a Systematic Theologian

In his *Peri Archon* (a systematic early work that was probably influenced by Greek philosophy), Origen had formulated the doctrine of a threefold sense of Scripture: by analogy with the tripartite constitution of man as body, mind and spirit, Sacred Scripture, too, has a physical, a psychic and a spiritual sense, to which the reader must advance by way of an ascending movement. De Lubac was able to demonstrate, however, that Origen most often does not follow his own schema in his commentaries and homilies, but rather follows the lead of Paul and the other New Testament writers who interpret the Old Testament in the light of Jesus Christ and take the Old Testament seriously as a witness to historical revelation, inquire into its deeper dimension as a witness to Christ and from this derive nourishment for the spiritual life. This presents a second threefold schema in competition with the first: the letter, the spirit and the moral sense (corresponding to history, faith and conduct).[3] Furthermore, this structure also corresponds to the true and complete act of faith, and not so much to the Platonic mysticism of ascent, which was always in danger of despising what is corporeal and earthly. If one combines these two concurrent schemas in Origen, the result

[3] See *HS*, pp. 204–22.

is the doctrine of the fourfold interpretation of Scripture; de Lubac identified Origen as the founder thereof.

A Synthetic Theory

The full significance of de Lubac's studies on scriptural interpretation becomes apparent against the background of an objective evaluation of so-called historical-critical exegesis. This sort of approach to the sources of the Christian faith had its beginnings in the sixteenth century. Its purpose, however, was not so much to prove the credibility of historical revelation as to discover, on the contrary, its relativity. Historical-critical research more often than not accepts as its premise a deist denial of the possibility of a historical revelation of God; it is accompanied by an interest in replacing the system of norms based on an appeal to divine revelation and warranted by the Church with an exclusively rationalistic morality and doctrine about God.

Whereas historical-critical exegesis swept triumphantly through nineteenth-century Protestant theology, the Catholic Magisterium remained aloof, well aware of the deficiencies, indeed, the destructive tendencies, of this new science. This led, on the other hand, to a narrow-minded perspective that for a long time allowed no place in Catholic theology for legitimate historical research into Scripture. The first encyclicals on the Bible, as well as the Responses of the Roman Biblical Commission, which was established in 1907, were to a great extent merely defensive and were criticized by Catholic exegetes as a hindrance to their work and an unlawful restriction of academic freedom.

It was a long time before historical Bible scholarship could be free of this mortgage. Even today, the relationship between dogmatic theology and exegesis is not without tensions. But twentieth-century theological work has contributed much toward a mutual understanding and the productive cooperation between exegesis and systematic theology. Now more than ever there is a pressing demand for a comprehensive theory that would describe how historical research into Sacred Scripture is compatible with and ordered to the theological investigation thereof, as well as to the application of Scripture in homilies and spiritual writing. This is all the more urgent, given the fact that, in reaction to a rationalistic exegesis of the Bible, other approaches to Scripture are now being offered, for instance, a deep-psychological approach, against which the Church's Magisterium has to defend the rights of historical research, precisely because the biblical testimony is not a mythical representation of timeless wisdom hidden in the human psyche but, rather, a witness to historical events.

Although the doctrine of the fourfold sense of Scripture, according to de Lubac, should not be revived in its classical form, its basic insight contains the way of solving the problem just described.

Adopted by the Church

Even though the Council does not expressly mention the doctrine of the fourfold sense of Scripture and also avoids the term *allegory*, it is nevertheless part of the background for article 12 of *Dei Verbum*, which calls for a synthesis of the historical approach to Scripture and the traditional interpretation of the Bible.

The doctrine has been adopted by the *Catechism of the Catholic Church* and has been rediscovered by Protestant theologians as well. The truth concealed within it absolutely must be carefully considered, says the New Testament scholar Hans

Hübner,[4] and the systematic theologian Wilfried Härle speaks of "the elements of truth in the doctrine of the fourfold sense of Scripture".[5]

[4] Hans Hübner, *Biblische Theologie als Hermeneutik* (1995), p. 286.
[5] Wilfried Härle, *Dogmatik* (1995), p. 130.

Hope instead of Utopia

There are two figures from the history of theology whom de Lubac has studied quite intensively: Origen and Joachim of Fiore. He had an extraordinary respect for Origen and, through his publications, to a great extent rehabilitated him. His relationship with Joachim of Fiore, on the other hand, is extremely ambivalent.

Joachim and the Third Kingdom of the Spirit

"O God, you revealed your glory to the three Apostles on Mount Tabor. At the same place you opened up to Blessed Joachim the truth of the Scriptures." So goes the concluding prayer on the memorial of Blessed Joachim of Fiore (May 29). The prayer refers to an event in his life and at the same time mentions the principal thought of his teaching: Joachim, who considered himself primarily as an explicator of the Sacred Scriptures, developed his theory from a particular view of the unity between the Old and New Testaments.

Who was Joachim of Fiore? Wherein lies his originality? What relevance does he have today, according to de Lubac?

Once the accounts of his life have been disentangled from legendary accretions, the following picture results. Joachim was born in Calabria around the year 1135. His father was a government official in the service of the Norman ruler of Sicily. After working for many years in a chancery in

Palermo—his father wanted to prepare him for a position as notary in the Norman royal court—Joachim set out on a journey to the East, which would be the great turning point in his life.

In the Holy Land, he visited the Eastern Rite monasteries at the Dead Sea and Jerusalem. Most important, however, he experienced upon Mount Tabor, which Tradition considers to be the site of the Transfiguration (see Mk 9:2ff.), a revelation concerning the meaning of Scripture, more particularly, concerning the correspondence between the Old and the New Testaments. After these experiences, he turned away from his worldly career and decided to live as a monk. Upon returning home, he entered the Cistercian monastery of Sambucina, near Luzzi. After a period of formation at several Cistercian monasteries, he ended up founding his own monastery, San Giovanni di Fiore, in the solitude of the Silla mountains in Calabria, so as to be able to devote himself completely and with even stricter asceticism to the contemplative life.[1] The order he founded spread through the foundation of daughter-houses and was approved by Pope Clement III, but it died out in the fifteenth century, whereupon the monasteries reverted to the Cistercian Order. In the year 1202, the theologian, founder and monastic reformer died; not only was he highly regarded by ecclesiastical dignitaries, but he was also esteemed by temporal rulers.

At the Lateran Council, in 1215, a polemical statement by Joachim was condemned; in it he argued against the Trinitarian teaching of Peter Lombard, reproaching him for

---

[1] The word *contemplation* is derived from Latin *contemplari*, "to survey, to consider carefully". The spiritual life is traditionally held to consist of the three steps of *lectio* (reading), *meditatio* (study) and *contemplatio*. Members of contemplative orders, unlike the "active" religious communities that perform charitable works, devote their lives entirely to prayer.

speaking about the divine nature in such a way that it was like a fourth divinity, a fourth Person.

Joachim proclaimed a third kingdom, a Kingdom of the Holy Spirit. According to his calculations, it was to be inaugurated around the year 1260 and would be accompanied by the dissolving of the Church's sacramental order and its replacement by a charismatic order, under the leadership of the monks; it would also be connected with the revelation of the "eternal Gospel", the announcement of which he saw in John's Apocalypse (Rev 14:6). Extremist groups affiliated with the mendicant orders that appeared in the thirteenth century viewed themselves as the fulfillment of Joachim's prophecies; their claims led to considerable unrest and divisive tendencies in the Church.

De Lubac demonstrated that the peculiar way in which Joachim of Fiore interpreted Scripture was the basis for his far-reaching theories, and he traced the tangled history of their influence down to modern times.

The Marxist philosopher Ernst Bloch was of the opinion that in Joachim of Fiore the typological and allegorical interpretation of Scripture found in the Church Fathers reached its culmination and perfection, and that Joachim was, so to speak, the executor of Origen's last will and testament. Upon superficial inspection, one might almost be inclined to agree with this evaluation. For Joachim does in fact use all the well-known terminology, such as allegory, typical sense, spiritual interpretation, spiritual understanding of Scripture. And yet in his hands the theology of Sacred Scripture expressed therein is transformed into something completely different.

In order to make clear the difference between his perspective and the theology of the Church Fathers, we must recall briefly the true meaning of patristic scriptural interpretation and the doctrine of the unity of Scripture as it was presented in the preceding chapter.[2]

Ever since the letters of Saint Paul, the allegorical interpretation of Scripture has not meant deriving arbitrary readings from biblical passages—or reading into them meanings that are not contained in the text at all. Rather, it means understanding the Old Testament in a Christological way. In practice, the allegorical method often consists of recognizing certain prefigurations (*typoi*) of Christ and the Church in the Old Testament and relating them to one another: Joseph in Egypt, Samson, Jonah, et al. are prefigurations of Christ. To this extent, typology and allegorical readings are not in opposition. In Christ, the letter of the Law has been transformed into the Spirit of the Gospel. The Law and the Prophets speak about Christ. Therefore, the Church Fathers were especially fond of seeing in the account of the Transfiguration a symbolic representation of the unity of Scripture that is mediated by Christ. On the mount of the Transfiguration, the glorified Christ appears between Moses and Elijah in the presence of three selected Apostles, Peter, James and John. Origen explains that if the Son of God was seen and contemplated in his glory, so that his face appeared like the sun and his clothing like light, then to the person who beholds Jesus in this state Moses likewise appears, that is, the Law, and with him Elijah also appears, and not just he, but all the prophets appear as well, in conversation with Jesus. But at the conclusion they saw only Jesus, that is, the Law and the Prophets have become clear in Jesus; he is the center of Scripture and the very essence of revelation.

---

[2] See Henri de Lubac, *Exégèse médiévale* (1959–1964) and *La Postérité spirituelle de Joachim de Fiore* (1979/1981). *Exégèse médiévale* has been translated into English: *Medieval Exegesis: The Four Senses of Scripture*, trans. Mark Sebanc, 2 vols. (Grand Rapids, Mich: Eerdmans, 1998).

Now Joachim too, in a vision that he had on the mount of the Transfiguration, was made privy to the understanding of Scripture that is alluded to in the prayer. In his principal work, *Liber concordiae novi ac veteris testamenti* (Book on the agreement between the Old and New Testament), Joachim elaborates his theory:

Every epoch of the Old Covenant corresponds to an epoch of the New Covenant, the time of Church's history. As a continuation of the doctrine of the seven ages of the world, which he correlates with the seven seals of the scroll from the Book of Revelation, Joachim distinguishes seven ages in the Old Covenant and seven in the New. His interpretation of the unity of Scripture is no longer concerned with showing how the Old and New Testaments both speak about one and the same Christ, although in different ways; rather, both the Old and the New Testaments are applied in a literal sense in order to interpret Church history and to predict future events. In this scheme, revelation is still incomplete. The fullness of revelation will come only with the "eternal Gospel", which will make possible a truly spiritual understanding thereof.

Transforming Augustine's threefold division of time—*ante legem* (the time before the promulgation of the Law), *sub lege* (the time under the Law) and *sub gratia* (the time of grace)—Joachim also speaks of three times or kingdoms: *sub lege, sub gratia* and *sub ampliori gratia* (the time of grace in greater fullness), whereby the time *sub lege* is the time of the Old Covenant (kingdom of the Father), the time *sub gratia* is the time of the Church (kingdom of the Son) and the third kingdom yet to come is that of the Holy Spirit.

With de Lubac we emphasize three points:

1. Joachim makes a radical break with the traditional understanding of the unity of Scripture. It no longer converges

on Christ as its one center, but rather consists in an external correlation of two historical sequences. In this theory, the spiritual understanding of Scripture is no longer the one made possible in the Church by the Spirit sent by Christ, but rather is expected in a future stage, in the time of the Holy Spirit. This is not a continuation of Origen's principles to their logical conclusion, but a completely new and divergent method.

2. The Christ-event and the sending of the Spirit lose their central importance in salvation history. Christ is reduced to a moment in history, alongside Abraham, Moses, Elijah, John the Baptist, Saint Benedict and Charlemagne. In principle, the time of Christ and of his Church can be surpassed in this world and will be replaced by the time of the Spirit.

3. While history loses its center in this way, it simultaneously is subsumed under the principle of progress.[3] The revelation of the Spirit and of his eternal Gospel will most surely come. The onset of this third kingdom will not be connected with a revolution, nor does it need to be brought about by human effort. We have only to wait calmly for it, and it will bring about a much deeper transformation of the spiritual man than any external reformation could ever accomplish. History is no longer the drama of salvation played out between Christ, the Lamb who was slain, and all those who belong to him on the one hand and the power of the Evil One on the other; instead, it is a continually advancing progress toward a kingdom of the Spirit. This is de Lubac's most serious objection: at the very least, Joachim has thereby

---

[3] Progress, considered absolutely, is not a Christian concept. Instead, there are always particular improvements in certain areas, which can be accompanied by retrograde developments in others. Making progress an ideological principle is contrary to faith in Christ, who is the center of history and the fullness of time.

thrown the switch that could send eschatological hope down the wrong track, toward a this-world utopia.

With his theories, Joachim of Fiore began two influential trends over the centuries. On the one hand, his brand of exegesis was imitated and continued, that is, scriptural interpretation as an attempt at making sense of history and foretelling the future. On the other hand, his theory of history itself had many different ramifications and brought forth many varieties of this-world utopian expectations. Gotthold Ephraim Lessing, for example, writes in his treatise *Erziehung des Menschengeschlechtes* [Education of the human race]: "It will come, certainly it will come, the age of perfection! It will come—the time of the New Gospel, the Eternal Gospel, which is promised to men in the very books of the New Covenant." The utopia took a disastrous turn in Marxism-Leninism, to which Joachim's thinking about history contributed after many metamorphoses and by way of Hegel's philosophy. The monks as the leading group are replaced here by the Communist Party as representatives of the working class. Since the Party knows the inevitable course of the historical process that leads to salvation, it may now resort as well to any and all means so as to eliminate those who stand in the way of this process.

According to de Lubac, the long-range consequences of Joachim's theory can be observed in the present-day Church also, in which it is not uncommon for individuals to dream dreams of another Church and to convert them into Church policy demands that would call into question the sacramental structure of the Church.

> Under the various forms it has assumed, I consider Joachimism to be a still-present and even pressing danger. I recognize it in the process of secularization, which, betraying the Gospel, transforms the search for that kingdom of God into social

utopias. I see it at work in what was so justly called the "self-destruction of the Church" [after Vatican II]. I believe that it can only increase the suffering and bring about the degradation of our humanity (*ASC*, pp. 156–57).

The Church is always a Church of sinners and of saints at the same time; be that as it may, the perpetual truth remains: Christ and his Holy Spirit cannot be separated from one another. Ever since Jesus was glorified, his Spirit has been sent to the Church. In this Spirit, the Church recognizes the salvific meaning of his life, death and Resurrection. In this Spirit, the Church recognizes the truth and the deeper spiritual meaning of the Scriptures. In this Spirit, who is poured out into our hearts, Christ sanctifies his Church in the Sacraments. The Spirit is the soul of the Church, which is simultaneously the People of God, the Body of Christ and the Temple of the Holy Spirit. De Lubac writes: "But in any case it must be said quite clearly, and in opposition to the illusions conjured up by promises of this kind, that the prophetic epoch is past. Today we have reality in our signs, and this state of affairs cannot be superseded as long as this world lasts. Insofar as we misinterpret this situation, we shall lapse from our condition of hope into mythology" (*SpCh*, p. 206). And the Eternal Gospel is no other Gospel than the Gospel of Christ, the interior contents of which will be fully disclosed to us when we shall have the privilege of seeing God face to face.

Origen and the "Last Things"

For many people even today, the name Origen is associated only with the doctrine of the *apokatastasis*, that is, the restoration of all things in the end times, when everyone shall be converted and saved. De Lubac was the first to attempt to

determine whether this really was Origen's teaching. The
controversial statements about a supposed universal salvation
are found in the systematic early work *Peri Archon* (1, 6),
which says that Christ will lead all creation back to the Father.
Then the question is posed to the reader: "Could not perhaps
the devils, too, be converted in the aeons to come, because of
their free will? Or does their wickedness, which is so in-
grained by long habit that it has become as it were second-
nature, prevent it? It is up to you, O Reader, to make the
judgment." Even if Origen himself perhaps would have liked
to answer the first question in the affirmative, he refrains from
making a declaration as to whether all shall really be saved or
not. De Lubac points out that in a passage where Origen had
the opportunity to apply his theory, namely, in connection
with the final fate of Judas, he is silent about whether the
apostle-turned-traitor may have been saved or damned. Therefore, Origen admits the possibility that a creature's freedom
can miss the mark after all. This is especially evident in
Origen's efforts to speak adequately about the so-called "last
things" (*eschata*). De Lubac shows in his analyses how subtly
and carefully Origen reflects the inadequacy of language and
of human ideas to give expression to the encounter with God
at the end of time as judgment, blessedness or hell [as the case
may be]. When Origen comments upon scriptural passages
that speak of warnings to sinners, future punishments or
rewards, he is guided by three concerns. First there is the
taunt of the pagan philosopher Celsus, that Christians imagine for themselves a God who is like an other-worldly torturer. Second, within the Church, Origen has to contend
with a kind of scriptural exegesis that takes every passage
literally. Finally, he strives, "by instructing his listeners about
the paths of divine pedagogy, to awaken and foster in them a
salutary uneasiness, without on the other hand neglecting to

lift up their hearts above merely servile fear" (p. 87).[4] Origen means to clarify our ideas about the last things and to show that the eternal blessings promised to the just do not consist of earthly pleasures granted eternally but, rather, in communion with God. Conversely, damnation is not being tormented in an other-worldly torture chamber but, rather (and this is much more horrible), the absence of God.

The most profound meaning of the fire metaphor is decisive in this connection. Origen insists: "The fire in question is not a kitchen fire, and God is not a torturer. This doubly coarse idea is an insult to God" (ibid., p. "91f."[GT]). Citing 1 Corinthians 3:13ff., Hebrews 10:27f. and then 1 Corinthians 2:9 as well, Origen sets forth the strictly personal meaning of all the biblical talk about "fire".

> In reality there is only one fire. Did not the Lord say [in effect in Exodus 3?], "Whoever draws near to me draws near to the fire"? Sacred Scripture confirms it: "Our God is a consuming fire"; the day of his coming is like a refiner's fire; he himself makes our whole being go through the crucible, so as to burn out all impurities or to make gold, silver and precious stones gleam brighter. The same fire of divinity produces in us opposite effects, corresponding to the state of our soul. Blessed are those who experience it as gentle and mild. God, while remaining himself the same, is simultaneously the fire of wrath and the fire of love" (ibid., pp. 93f.).

For Origen there is no doubt: divine wrath exists, yet it is different from human wrath. It is God's holiness, which manifests itself as wrath to the sinner who refuses to turn to God. In all of God's "threats", we can hear also the voice of his mercy and his love for his creatures, which is striving

---

[4] Henri de Lubac, "Tu m'as trompé, Seigneur" (1979); Rudolf Voderholzer is quoting the German edition, "Du hast mich betrogen, Herr!" (1984). Page numbers are from that edition.—ED.

after love in return. After the threats and after the promises, however, comes the hour of silence, "the silence that is more marvelous than the most magnificent promises, more terrible than the most formidable warnings" (ibid., p. 96). What no eye has seen and no ear has heard, what the heart of man has not conceived: this applies both to the great things that God prepares for those who love him as well as to what those who refuse to have anything to do with God prepare for themselves. "Much more than evil, pure and simple, the only thing to fear is being forgotten by God" (ibid., p. 97).

Thus de Lubac was able to show that Origen had already developed what in contemporary theology is considered to be the principle of a doctrine concerning the understanding of eschatological statements: "God is the 'last thing' of the creature. Gained, he is heaven; lost, he is hell; examining, he is judgment; purifying, he is purgatory." [5]

---

[5] Hans Urs von Balthasar, *Verbum caro* (1960); English edition *Explorations in Theology*, vol. 1, *The Word Made Flesh* (San Francisco: Ignatius Press, 1989), p. 260.

Mysticism

The central inspiration of de Lubac's theology is his unwritten book on Christian mysticism. Talk about mysticism recurs throughout his writings like a *leitmotiv*. De Lubac has a mystical understanding of Christianity.

Mysticism is a shimmering concept. Many contemporaries associate it with extraordinary visions, special charisms, experiences of union with God and perhaps also, by way of negative theology, with the sense of the radical otherness of God and the painful experience of his absence in the "dark night of the soul" (John of the Cross).

De Lubac does know about these special forms of experiencing God, and he cites again and again the appropriate testimonies. Yet he seems to be more concerned with making mysticism comprehensible as a form of personal acceptance and assimilation of the faith as a relationship with God the Father, mediated by Christ and sustained in the Holy Spirit—something that is fundamentally possible and even necessary for all baptized and confirmed Christians. Although he did not manage to produce a systematic presentation of Christian mysticism, we do have something like a sketch that was written by de Lubac.[1]

[1] Henri de Lubac, "Christliche Mystik in Begegnung mit den Weltreligionen" [Christian mysticism in its encounter with world religions], in J. Sudbrack, ed., *Das Mysterium und die Mystik: Beiträge zu einer Theologie der christlichen Gotteserfahrung* (1974), pp. 77–110. Here cited as *Mystic.*

The point of departure for de Lubac's reflections is the talk about mysticism in other world religions as well and the opinion that the "mystical" is the common denominator of all religions.

De Lubac cites a certain René Daumal: "I read one after the other texts about Bhakti, quotations from Hasidic writers and a passage from Francis of Assisi. To that I add a few of Buddha's sayings and am once again impressed by the fact that it is all the same" (*Mystik*, p. 85).

Opposed to this is the perspective that says "Outside the Church there is no mysticism." According to this view, mysticism is always connected with ecclesiastical life, nourished by meditation on Sacred Scripture and by the sacraments.

According to de Lubac, we must go beyond both of the aforementioned theses. De Lubac is acquainted with the variety and wealth of religious experience in mankind: "The more one looks at the history of spirituality, the more mysticism appears to be, by its very essence, a universal affair. It also develops outside of the positive religions" (ibid., p. 81). De Lubac raises the question whether it might not be possible to speak even about an atheistic mysticism, for instance, when Nietzsche says of himself, "I am a mystic and believe in nothing!" Mysticism is fascinating, and mysticism is not limited to the province of the Church. The Church herself admits, according to de Lubac, that men can receive grace from God even outside the visible Church and can be led on to mystical experiences. Although, as Christians understand it, mysticism is normally bound up with the life of faith and the sacraments, one cannot say that there is no mysticism at all outside the Church.

Yet, on the other hand, de Lubac asks the reader to consider that whenever someone maintains that all mystical experiences are alike, this results from a superficial analysis of texts taken out of their spiritual context and from a disregard of the real differences between the individual religions (ibid., p. 86).

De Lubac's solution is related to his understanding of human nature as a limitless openness to God: "Mystical striving is something innate in human nature, for man is designed for this union. In other words: man is capable of assimilating the mystery."

This striving for God, which is given as part of man's nature yet originates from God, finds the most varied expressions in the religions of mankind. This "mystical inclination" can become stunted, it can misunderstand itself, it can turn into protest and hostility. But it can never be entirely denied. The decisive question is whether or not a personal encounter is presupposed in the mystical experience. "The real deception occurs (and errors and falsifications follow) when someone thinks that he has found or hopes to find the encounter—or at least what one views as fulfillment—in this neutral capability alone. Yet in and of itself it has no driving force and is only an empty openness. This openness can be understood correctly only in its relation to the Mystery" (ibid., p. 89).

In the God-man Jesus Christ, the Christian message reveals to man the final truth about himself and thus elevates the mystical inclination of human nature, purifies it and brings it to its true fulfillment. In pre- and non-Christian mysticism, there is a great danger of interpreting the search itself as fulfillment and of imagining an encounter for oneself. Left to its own devices, however, this natural mysticism is ultimately sterile. Fulfillment must come from a real encounter. Every genuine mysticism is, in the final analysis, not active but passive, has something to do with "suffering", with the experience of a personal encounter of "being with" another person. Conversely, it is true that "[W]hen the human spirit believes that it possesses fullness, then its emptiness is no

longer curable" (Auguste Valensin, cited in *Mystik*, p. 89).
When "mysticism" acknowledges no encounter, "it becomes
in some form or other a self-contained mystical contemplation and experience, with no Mystery, satisfied with itself—
which in our opinion is the most logically consistent form of
atheism" (*Mystik*, p. 90).

Essential to de Lubac's understanding of mysticism is the
relation between mysticism and Mystery. "Christian mysticism does not withdraw from the faith, rather it is inherent
in the logic of the life of faith" (*Mystik*, p. 90). Although
relatively successful forms of mysticism can exist outside the
boundaries of the visible Church, it is still true from the
perspective of the faith, once it has been received, that "[o]ut-
side of the Mystery, as it is received in faith, all mysticism
ceases or becomes distorted" (ibid., p. 91). In other words:
"Mysticism interiorizes the Mystery; it owes its life to the
mystery and in turn keeps it alive" (ibid.).

The Mystery, however, is not a tenet or a truth, but a
Person: Jesus Christ. And just as all the mysteries of the
Christian faith are connected with God's self-communication
in Jesus Christ and derive from it their unity and coherence,
so too can we say that all Christian mysticism, which is to be
understood in terms of the Mystery, is contained in Christ.
Citing Divo Barsotti, de Lubac says,

> The Mystery is Christ in you (Col 1:27). Because it is the
> revelation of God's love, it constitutes all of theology. Be-
> cause it is the action of God, who humbles himself and
> becomes man, it establishes Christian worship, it is the Mys-
> tery of faith. Because it is the action of man, who strives to
> live according to God's will, all of mysticism lies enclosed
> within it. All revelation is given to us in Christ, the pioneer
> and perfecter of our faith, as it is written in the Letter to
> the Hebrews [12:2]. All worship is perfected in the unique

sacrifice of Christ, and all mysticism consists of perfecting Christ's life in us (*Mystik*, p. 90).

Friendship with Jesus Christ

The Christian experience of God is not only participation in Jesus' experience of God, but also gravitates toward his Person and consists of friendship with him. On this point, all the great theologians, most of whom are also honored as saints, reach an agreement. The true beginning of being a Christian, and hence the first thing needed to overcome the crisis in the Church, "is love for Jesus Christ. This love makes a person a Christian. . . . This will never change."[2] De Lubac sees Origen, Bernard, Augustine, Thomas Aquinas, Möhler, Newman, and others as agreeing on this personal understanding of the faith. It is a personalism "which the first Apostles, especially the Apostle Paul, professed and which so many Saints, so many simple Christians lived without intellectual presumption" (ibid., p. 44).

This Christological orientation was for de Lubac, even before any theological reflection, first and foremost an experience of faith. The spirituality of the Jesuit Order helped him to learn and practice friendship with Jesus.

Part and parcel of this is a special respect for the Name of Jesus; January 1, the Feast of the Holy Name of Jesus, is, after all, the name day of the Jesuits. This explains even more profoundly de Lubac's felicitous observation that Origen (long before Bernard of Clairvaux and Bernardine of Siena) was already acquainted with a specific devotion to the Name of Jesus. For example, in his commentary on the Book of

[2] Henri de Lubac, *L'Église dans la crise actuelle* (1969); see the German edition, *Krise zum Heil?*, p. 43. (Page numbers for this work reference the German edition.—ED.)

Joshua, he celebrates the first mention of the name and emphasizes that in all of biblical tradition there is no sinner who bore that name (see *HS*, p. 63).

Thus Christian mysticism has nothing to do with an "inward flight" from the world; rather, it is a matter of interiorizing one's imitation of Christ.

The Spiritual and Mystical Interpretation of Scripture

Historians expend much effort to reclaim the Old Testament Song of Songs as an Oriental love poem with an unabashed view of love and sexuality, to show that it is nothing more than such a lyrical composition and to rescue it from the allegedly distorted interpretations of the spiritual tradition.

Equipped with the criteria for making distinctions provided by the doctrine of the fourfold sense of Scripture, we can and must always recognize and admit that these literary texts originated in a profane setting. Yet even a historical hermeneutic will soon run up against the fact that these texts owe their place in the canon of Sacred Scripture solely thanks to the fact that in biblical times they were already understood in a figurative sense also as the expression of the loving relationship between Yahweh and his bride, the People of Israel.

And so it was simply continuing along the lines of the traditional biblical understanding of Scripture when Christian commentators on the texts of the Old Covenant meditated on the soul's relationship to Jesus and derived from it nourishment for their faith. Of course, these interpretations are anything but historical commentaries. When Saint Bernard of Clairvaux[3] links extensive spiritual considerations to

---

[3] St. Bernard of Clairvaux (1090–1153), the most important theologian and mystic of the Cistercian Order, was Abbot of Clairvaux from 1115. The twelfth century has been described as the century of St. Bernard. Preeminent

every single verse in the Song of Songs, he is taking the text as the point of departure for a portrayal of his own spiritual experience. But these interpretations are not intended to be scriptural commentaries, nor do they make such commentaries superfluous. Recall once more de Lubac's admonition: no false alternatives! Theology and the Church need both. As necessary as historical research is, theology deprives itself of a valuable source for its spirituality and mysticism when it looks down on these testimonies of the spiritual tradition (see *SpCh*, pp. 362–64).

On the Feast of the Presentation of the Lord, in 1931, de Lubac professed his solemn vows as a member of the Society of Jesus. His attitude, with which he followed the path of imitating Christ, is expressed in the prayer *Suscipe*, which Saint Ignatius composed and which summarizes Ignatian mysticism:

Take, O Lord, and receive all my liberty,
my memory, my understanding and my entire will,
all that I have and possess.
You have given all to me,
to You, O Lord, I return it.
All is Yours; dispose of it according to Your will.
Give me Your love and Your grace,
for this is enough for me.

among Bernard's writings are his treatise *On the Love of God* and his mystical-allegorical *Sermons on the Song of Songs*. Beginning in 1970, a series of scholarly annotated editions of Bernard's works was published by Cistercian Publications, Spencer, Mass.

SUGGESTED READINGS

Introduction to Henri de Lubac

A review of his life and work is provided by the following:

de Lubac, Henri. *At the Service of the Church: Henri de Lubac Reflects on the Circumstances That Occasioned His Writings.* Translated by Anne Elizabeth Englund. Communio Books/Ignatius Press, San Francisco, 1993. Originally published as *Mémoire sur l'occasion de mes écrits.* 1989; 2nd ed. 1992.

De Lubac comments on Vatican II and its effects on Church history in two books:

de Lubac, Henri. *L'Église dans la crise actuelle.* 1969. An abridged English version is available: "The Church in Crisis". *Theology Digest* 17 (1969): 312–25.

———. *De Lubac: A Theologian Speaks.* Interview conducted by Angelo Scola. Los Angeles: Twin Circle Pub. Co., 1985. This is an abridged translation of *Entretien autour de Vatican II: Souvenirs et Réflexions.* Paris: Catholique-Cerf, 1985.

A Portrait of Henri de Lubac

An expert survey of his complete works is the following:

Balthasar, Hans Urs von. *The Theology of Henri de Lubac: An Overview.* Translated by Joseph D. Fessio, S.J., Michael M. Waldstein and Susan Clements. San Francisco: Ignatius Press, 1991. Originally published as *Henri de Lubac: Sein organisches Lebenswerk.* Einsiedeln: Johannes Verlag, 1976.

[See also:]

Russo, Antonio. *Henri de Lubac* (in Italian). 1994.

Beginning to Read Henri de Lubac

de Lubac, Henri. *Catholicism: Christ and the Common Destiny of Man.* Translated by Lancelot C. Sheppard and Elizabeth Englund. San Francisco: Ignatius Press, 1988. Originally published as *Catholicisme: Les aspects sociaux du dogme.* 1938.

———. *The Christian Faith: An Essay on the Structure of the Apostles' Creed.* Translated by Richard Arnandez. San Francisco: Ignatius Press, 1986. Originally published as *La Foi chrétienne: Essai sur la structure du Symbole des Apôtres.* 1970.

———. *The Church: Paradox and Mystery.* Translated by James R. Dunne. New York: Alba House, 1969. Originally published as *Paradoxe et Mystère de l'Église.* 1967.

———. *Paradoxes of Faith.* San Francisco: Ignatius Press, 1987. Reprint of *Paradoxes.* Translated by Paule Simon and Sadie Kreilkamp. South Bend, Ind.: Fides Publishers, 1948. Along with the companion volume: *More paradoxes.* Translated by Anne Englund Nash. San Francisco: Ignatius Press, 2002. Originally published as one volume: *Paradoxes suivi de nouveaux paradoxes.* 1959.

Works by Henri de Lubac on Particular Subjects

de Lubac, Henri. *Augustinianism and Modern Theology.* Translated by Lancelot Sheppard. New York: Herder and Herder, 1969. Originally published as *Augustinisme et Théologie moderne.* 1965.

———. *A Brief Catechesis on Nature and Grace.* Translated by Richard Arnandez. San Francisco: Ignatius Press, 1984. Originally published as *Petite catéchèse sur Nature et Grâce.* Paris, 1980.

———. *Corpus mysticum: L'Eucharistie et l'Église au Moyen Âge, Étude historique.* Paris: Aubier, 1944.

———. *The Discovery of God.* Translated by Alexander Dru. Grand Rapids, Mich.: W. B. Eerdmans Pub. Co., 1996. Originally published as *De la connaissance de Dieu.* 1945. Rev. ed. *Sur les chemins de Dieu.* 1956

———. *The Drama of Atheist Humanism.* Translated by Edith M. Riley. New York: Sheed & Ward, 1950. Translated by Anne Englund Nash and Mark Sebanc. San Francisco: Ignatius Press,

1995. Originally published as *Le Drame de l'humanisme athée*. 1944.

———. *History and Spirit: The Understanding of Scripture according to Origen*. San Francisco: Ignatius Press, 2007. Originally published as *Histoire et Esprit: L'Intelligence de l'Écriture d'après Origène*. 1950.

———. *The Mystery of the Supernatural*, translated by Rosemary Sheed, Herder and Herder, New York, 1967. Originally published as *Le Mystère du Surnaturel*. 1965.

———. *The Splendor of the Church*. Translated by Michael Mason. New York: Sheed & Ward, 1956. Reprinted by Ignatius Press, 1986, 1999. Originally published as *Méditation sur l'Église*. 1953.

———. *Scripture in the Tradition*. Translated by Luke O'Neill. New York: Crossroad Pub., 2000. Reprint of *The Sources of Revelation*. Herder and Herder, 1968. Originally published as *L'Écriture dans la Tradition*. 1966. This latter volume is an abridgment of the multi-volume *Medieval Exegesis*. Translated by Mark Sebanc [vol. 1] and E. M. Macierowski [vol. 2]. Grand Rapids, Mich.: W. B. Eerdmans Pub. Co., 1998, 2000.

———. *Theology in History:* vol. 1, *The Light of Christ*; vol. 2, *Disputed Questions and Resistance to Nazism*. Translated by Anne Englund Nash. San Francisco: Ignatius Press. 1996. Originally published as *Théologie dans l'histoire*, I: *La Lumière du Christ*, and II: *Questions disputées et résistance au nazisme* (1990).

———. "Tu m'as trompé, Seigneur!": Le commentaire d'Origène sur Jérémie 20:7. [You have deceived me, Lord: Origen's commentary on Jer 20:7]. In *Mémorial Joseph Chaine*. Lyons: Faculté catholique, 1950. Reprinted in *Recherches dans la foi: Trois études sur Origène, Saint Anselme, et la philosophie chrétienne*. . Paris: Beauchesne, 1979. Pp. 9–78.

Studies about Henri de Lubac

Figura, Michael. *Der Anruf der Gnade: Über die Beziehung des Menschen zu Gott nach Henri de Lubac*. 1979.

Lenk, Martin. *Von der Gotteserkenntnis: Natürliche Theologie im Werk Henri de Lubacs*. 1993.

Voderholzer, Rudolf. *Die Einheit der Schrift und ihr geistiger*

Sinn: Der Beitrag Henri de Lubacs zur Erforschung von Geschichte und Systematik christlicher Bibelhermeneutik. 1998.

Complete Works

A complete listing of publications by Henri de Lubac up to the year 1974 is contained in Karl Heinz Neufeld and Michel Sales, *Bibliographie Henri de Lubac S.J. (1925–1974)* (1974). Supplemental listings until the year 1989 are given in Henri de Lubac, *Théologie dans l'histoire,* vol. 2.

A critical edition of the complete works of de Lubac is being published by:

Association Internationale Cardinal Henri de Lubac
128, rue Blomet
F-75015 Paris

Jaca Books in Milan, Italy, has published de Lubac's works in Italian.